EASY

STEPS

FOR

LEARNING

Improve Your Learning Ability
and Daily Functioning Skills

Jen McCall

Copyright © 2020 Jen McCall

Published by
Kindle Direct Publishing
Subsidiary of Amazon.com

DEDICATION

For students and teachers,

roles performed by everyone.

CONTENTS

INTRODUCTION

Students cannot read, write and think well enough in higher education, teachers are saying. They cannot present adequate explanation about what they have learned from reading, and they cannot analyze and evaluate material to develop personal opinions for writing. Strategies in this guide can solve these problems with effective note writing for the analysis of reading material and for critical thinking, also for easily planning writing with efficient steps that create your own unique structure of topics to organize material when planning writing.

Many smart students are not going to college because they are afraid of failure and getting low grades. Students are failing to develop effective learning strategies during their education. Meanwhile the demand is increasing for effective learning skills, both for education and work, and will continue to increase in the future. Teachers are often failing to promote effective learning skills because they lack sufficient strategies for teaching high quality learning skills. Both students and teachers need more effective strategies that promote their best functioning.

Studying and teaching depend upon interrelated strategies. Teachers should know about the best study strategies so they can choose assignments that provide practice with important learning skills. Advanced students should know how to plan any course of study so they can understand how to achieve their own learning goals efficiently. Also you might be planning a home study program for yourself or someone else, so you should know the basic steps for planning a course of study.

Would you like to study and think better? to easily write long essays and research papers? to organize planning and time by using business procedures? to plan better quality study at home like a professional teacher? and choose your educational goals with orientation information about work? This guide helps with the problems of both learning and teaching study skills. It's for students who want better grades, for parents and teachers who want to help children learn and for anyone seeking better skills. Study steps in this guide represent important fundamental skills that everyone wants for their everyday functioning.

1 STUDYING AND THINKING

Study Steps

SUMMARIZE the key concepts or strategy and list the key points supporting the central message

ANALYZE by outlining all levels of topics and supporting points in study material

EVALUATE pros and cons of supporting material for the topic, subtopics and paragraph topics

STUDY IS ANALYSIS

Simple reading might get you through high school and college, but with an inadequate performance and unnecessary struggle. Although you could struggle through higher levels of education, then you may lack sufficient skills for the higher levels of work. Good strategies are essential to improve learning performance. First you need good grades in high school to get into the college of your choice. Then you need good grades in college to get into higher educational programs in college. Also if you want to work in high level careers with good performance, you must develop effective reading, writing and thinking skills.

Often students remember only a few interesting points after reading something, or else they might not remember anything. Teachers say that it's inadequate for study, and that students don't understand the study material well enough. You need a strategy to identify and keep track of important points with their supporting points in your study material. This provides a means of efficient review and thinking so you can reach higher quality educational achievement, perform the higher levels of work and also improve your everyday functioning.

Simple reading often fails to promote sufficient thinking for the higher levels of learning. The problem is that you might not notice enough or think about key topics and relationships that are important to reach adequate understanding for your goals. Simple reading tends to cause partial learning with memorizing only a few interesting points and facts to pass tests. You might not think about the important key points and their supporting points if you're unaware of the value in examining these qualities for greater understanding of reading material.

Studying is best defined as analysis or else applying suitable forms and levels of thinking to reach high quality understanding. Analysis requires suitable strategies to promote comprehensive understanding and adequate memory with your study material. Analysis includes developing the critical thinking skills required for excellent performance with many higher level learning and functioning activities. Your best quality of learning isn't simply about gaining general knowledge. Also it's about analyzing, evaluating and applying knowledge so that you achieve higher levels of understanding and functioning.

Analyzing the key points and relationships in study material with note writing can increase your understanding and memory. Generally the quantity of your study material will be too large to process easily, so you might not focus sufficiently on the most important points and relationships in material unless you write notes to keep track of the organizing topics.

Note writing is your essential tool for mentally processing material for all kinds of thinking goals and practical applications. Many thinking activities require suitable note writing to improve performance, and note writing improves your quality of learning. Choose suitable note patterns to reach the quality of analysis and thinking you want for your material and learning goals.

Apply note writing with flexibility according to how thoroughly you want to study and the quantity of your time. You don't have to study everything in the same way. Sometimes you only need to underline a few points or write a brief summary, and at other times you need to write a complete outline and organize various note patterns to fully analyze and evaluate material. Sometimes you need to continue analyzing material in many different ways to explore complex interrelationships and also to evaluate the suitability of material for your interests and applications.

When you learn about the note writing strategies for learning, you can choose the most effective patterns for your material and goals. However the following levels of thinking and analysis are always important for excellent learning, and you can consistently apply these levels better with note writing.

STEPS FOR ANALYSIS AND THINKING

Six Levels of Knowledge and Thinking

The following levels of mental activity have been identified by Benjamin Bloom:

Knowledge - becoming acquainted with information and ideas
Comprehension - developing good understanding about study material
Analysis - studying relationships among organizational levels and units of material
Synthesis - reorganizing and combining information and ideas into new relationships
Evaluation - judging accuracy, value and usefulness of material
Application – considering the practical uses of material

Use these levels to improve your quality of learning:

STUDY STEPS

Organize – by identifying the organization of topics in material to improve your understanding and memory
Summarize – by listing the central concepts or strategy and the key points supporting the central topic
Analyze – by listing the levels of topics and listing their levels of supporting points

ANALYSIS STEPS

Summary – list key points or subtopics for the central topic, and list supporting points for these subtopics
Outline – organizing the levels of topics with their supporting points
Diagram – organizing the complex patterns of relationships in highly detailed material

THINKING STEPS

Evaluate – by examining supporting material for the key points or subtopics and paragraph topics
Synthesize –by reorganizing units of material to promote more thinking and new perspectives
Apply – by considering the quality of material for your practical applications and goals

Six levels of knowledge and thinking can help you write notes that improve your quality of thinking with higher level learning. The first two thinking levels can be applied by summarizing and organizing, since these activities are the basic techniques used for gaining adequate comprehension from your reading material. Use the note patterns of summary, outline and diagram to reach adequate analysis for study. Use the thinking levels of synthesis, evaluation and application to reach higher level critical thinking for discussion and for better quality essays and research papers. Higher levels of analysis and thinking indicate that learning can be more than simply reciting material from memory.

STUDY STEPS

Organize, Summarize, Analyze

Change simple reading into effective studying by writing notes for the first three thinking levels. Organizing, summarizing and analyzing are basic study techniques that help you reach better understanding and memory. You can perform these levels of thinking by writing summary notes about your study material. Summary notes are the first level of analysis, and they help you think about the central topic and key concept(s) before applying additional levels of outline analysis.

When you don't notice enough about the concepts and topics in study material, you tend to remember random information with poor quality understanding. Your explanation of material presents only partial perspective and is lacking comprehensive understanding. Solve this problem by writing summary notes to clarify the key organizing concepts in study material and you will also remember more of the supporting points.

Write a summary about each chapter of study material to create review notes about key concepts and subtopics. Summary notes can help you identify and keep track of the organizing concepts and topics, so you can evaluate the quality of supporting material. Summary notes help you understand reading material more fully and they help you keep track of the concepts and subtopics with their supporting points that you need to think about.

List the important concepts and topics you want to remember and think about from reading material. Note writing helps you keep track of key points and keeps your focus during reading. Your notes can help you see the organization of material and they provide easy review for thinking and memory. If you can't remember enough about the key concepts and topics, your study is lacking effectiveness for higher level learning.

Too many students don't notice the concepts and key points during reading, and they don't remember enough of these key points unless they are writing summary notes and reviewing their notes occasionally. The solution is writing a list or simple outline of the most important points that you want to review and think about from your reading. Without note writing, you tend to remember only partial information instead of an adequate and reasonably comprehensive summary. This is generally viewed as poor quality understanding and learning.

Reading for casual interests is different than reading for good quality learning. Casual reading is enjoyable and you may tend to understand enough for casual interests. Reading for higher level learning requires more comprehensive understanding and memory of important points. Also higher level study material is more difficult to process and remember. Before your reading, decide how thoroughly you want to understand and process the material, so you can write suitable notes to reach your goals for sufficient understanding and academic performance.

Students lack adequate focus upon concepts and topics from reading unless they write summary notes and review them occasionally. Many students don't perform well with discussion, written essays and the evaluation of reading material unless they have organized the supporting points for the concepts and key study topics. If you can identify the central concepts or strategy and list their supporting points or subtopics, write it in the form of summary notes that you can easily review and remember.

Research on learning found that students performed better on achievement tests when they only read summaries instead of the whole textbook (McKeachie 150). But you can perform even better by reading the whole text and writing good summaries. Summarizing requires the activities of sorting, organizing and thinking about the material. These activities help you focus on the organizing structure in material, and they provide review notes so you can continue with higher quality thinking.

Poor quality learning consists of only memorizing information, while good quality learning consists of thinking about the topics and relationships. Although most teachers won't expect you to remember large quantities of detail from your study material, you should be prepared to discuss the concepts and topics, also their supporting points and share your opinions. Therefore you need to write notes about the basic organizing structure of topics and supporting points to improve understanding and thinking, so you can prepare for advanced learning activities such as higher quality discussion, reciting and writing.

Writing a Chapter Summary

The typical chapter contains six large points on the average, it has been observed. You can capture these key points by writing summary notes. Written material is organized by arranging units of material into levels of topics followed by lower levels of their supporting points. Writing summary notes about this organizing structure can improve understanding and memory significantly. It's important to capture key concepts and topics in material and their supporting points. This creates summary notes that make more sense and are easier to remember than simply listing the topic of each paragraph for a memorable point.

It has been observed that all textbook material contains large points, supporting points and transitions. Therefore if you sort and organize the largest key points with their supporting points, you can essentially capture the central concept and message, creating excellent notes for review. Concepts are generalized ideas that provide orientation for mentally processing lower level material. The large organizing concepts in a message are useful for evaluating the quality of topics and supporting points.

Research on learning shows it's important to see summary and organization for adequate understanding of reading material (McKeachie 229, 238). Therefore you need a strategy that helps you process study material for these qualities. The best strategy begins with writing a summary about the organizing concepts and key points and arranging the supporting points for these points. Then you might consider writing notes for additional analysis, such as fully outlining the levels of topics and their supporting points when this is useful for your thinking goals.

A summary is easier to remember than a full outline, so it's more effective for your general orientation. At least write a list of the key points you want to remember, then you might outline additional material for your thinking goals. An outline provides more levels of organization, so an outline is more effective when you want to identify supporting points for more levels of topics. When you list or outline the organizing structure in material for easy review, it helps you think about and remember important key points and even more detailed supporting material.

Pay attention to meaningful titles and your reading material makes more sense. Meaningful titles and subtitles usually show important topics and points, so they help you understand the organizing structure of the material. Don't assume that titles are subtopics, but always sort reading material to be sure that you have clearly identified the most important concepts and their supporting points. It's much easier to pay attention to titles and subtitles when writing notes about the organizing points.

Summarizing improves your functioning with many activities. When you're telling a long and complex story, first summarize the story. When you're presenting classroom lessons or making business phone calls, begin speaking with summaries and end with summaries. After watching visual demonstrations or hearing verbal explanations, summarize the material since this improves your understanding and memory. You can greatly increase the effectiveness of your learning and communication by beginning and ending with summaries for most activities.

Skimming and Summarizing

Worthwhile material might be obtained from books and articles without reading whole books and articles. Simply use skimming and summarizing to take notes about material of interest. Also this strategy is valuable if you want to research large quantities of information without fully reading many books and articles.

Some books are only to be tasted, others nibbled, and others chewed and digested. You can identify these options for yourself when you preview books. When sorting books in a bookstore or library, use the preview technique of skimming and summarizing to see if you're interested in reading the books more thoroughly. Skimming and summarizing helps you preview material to gain access to much larger quantities of information. Most people use skimming, but they could be using summarizing better to gain more information. The strategies of skimming and summarizing can help you gain easy access to more information.

Skimming is useful to sort for details and summary points. Begin looking for an introduction to the central concept and supporting subtopics for your general orientation. Read the title, subtitles and first sentence of each paragraph, which is often a topic sentence. Or else you might simply browse for general understanding before identifying the central concepts and their supporting subtopics. When written material is reasonably well organized you can easily find the most important points, and you can take notes about points of interest to increase your thinking and memory by reviewing your notes.

When previewing new material, you can learn faster and with greater efficiency by skimming and summarizing and by writing summary notes about material of interest. Otherwise you might remember very little if you don't summarize. This phenomenon is observed in many informal learning occasions, such as hearing a speech or watching TV. When you speak or write a summary of material, it improves your understanding, memory and quality of thinking. Skimming and summarizing are important techniques that enable you to gain access to greater quantities of valuable and interesting information.

ANALYSIS STEPS

Summary, Outline, Diagram

Your highest level reading skill requires comprehensive analysis of material. Perform this kind of analysis with an outline showing the fundamental levels of organization in written material: topic or concept, subtopics and paragraph topics. This outline should show the structure of key points with their supporting points to increase your understanding and memory of material.

Note patterns below are the most commonly used for analysis of study material, but you can use many other variations of note patterns for additional forms of thinking.

Summary – list the key points supporting the central topic and list their supporting points

Outline – write notes to organize the levels of topics along with their supporting points

Diagram – organize complex patterns of relationships in highly detailed material

You need to understand the big picture, the mid-level picture and also patterns of relationships in highly detailed material for comprehensive analysis of reading material. Three kinds of outline notes are useful to fully analyze material. The first level is a summary of the key concept(s) or strategy. This consists of identifying central concept(s) along with their supporting points. The second most common level of analysis is listing the central topic and subtopics with their supporting paragraph topics.

Comprehensive analysis of study material may require an outline showing the levels of topics and supporting points more fully than the first two levels of outlines. Fully analyze material by outlining more levels of the topics with supporting points. Sometimes you need to think about more levels of structure depending on the study material and your goals. Fully outlining material shows all levels of topics with their supporting points.

Examine complex patterns of relationships within technical material by using various forms of diagramming. These note patterns are useful for the analysis of highly detailed material. For example when studying math, it's important to notice steps for solving complex numerical relationships. When studying law, you must focus on details of sentence structure and grammar since these qualities affect the precise meaning of laws and contracts. When studying science, it's important to notice details about scientific terminology and formulas.

Focus your attention on key points and organization of topics in study material. This helps with understanding more fully and helps with remembering more material. Also this helps with thinking and evaluating the pros and cons of supporting points. Using the outline structure below helps you identify key points and organization. When you outline important key points with their supporting points, this improves your understanding of the material, while it provides better quality review for thinking and memory. Notes about the organization of topics in material helps to keep your focus, promoting greater learning.

You can simply list the most interesting or valuable points you find in reading material, or you can also list the subtopics with their levels of supporting points. Then you may show how your most important or interesting points are supported by the subtopics and their supporting paragraph topics.

Outline for Analyzing Reading
This three level outline is equally effective for analyzing reading material and for planning writing

Topic   **Title for Concept**
   Subtopics   **Key Points**
     Paragraph Topics   **Supporting Points**

List the key points and organize their supporting points in your study material. This helps with thinking and evaluating the quality of material. The central concept or topic of material is supported by the key points or subtopics, and paragraph topics organize the supporting material for each of these subtopics. This three level outline is equally effective for planning writing. List your key points about the topic first into a writing outline, and organize supporting material into paragraph topics.

Using this three level outline for study notes helps you solve the following problems with reading for learning.

1) Understanding is greater with your outline analysis.
When you list the basic structure of topics and supporting points in reading material, it provides better quality understanding.

2) Thinking is higher level with evaluation of material.
When you can easily review the topics and supporting points, it helps you evaluate the quality of supporting material for topics.

3) Memory is improved with your review and thinking.
When you review and think about the levels of topics, you can remember more of the topics and their supporting points.

Three levels of outline patterns are useful to analyze material for comprehensive understanding and for evaluating the quality of your study material. First summarize the largest concept(s) with their supporting points or subtopics. Often you need the three level outline pattern showing the subtopics along with their supporting paragraph topics. Then you might use more levels of outline, depending on your study material and goals. Generally you need different note patterns for technical material and math than you would use for analysis of social science material.

The outline pattern has been around a long time for study, but lacking sufficient strategy for learning better with an outline. Students often write poor quality outlines and notes for review. Simple outlining might not be meaningful enough when the material is poorly organized. Reading material may be too poorly organized to outline easily. You might need to create your own versions of outline patterns showing the key points or subtopics for sufficient analysis of material. Generally, you need to see the largest points or strategy with supporting points for subtopics, and then supporting points for the paragraph topics.

You can develop greater critical thinking skills over time with note writing that helps you mentally process study material. Writing a list, outline and other forms of note patterns promotes greater understanding and thinking about your reading material. Writing suitable outline notes to process material helps you read smarter, because the material makes more sense by identifying the organizing structure of topics. Then using your structure notes for review and thinking promotes greater understanding and thinking that's required for higher levels of learning.

Complex detailed technical material might not make sense unless you organize notes that analyze the detailed patterns of relationships to provide greater perspective for understanding. Also you need to look at the summary pattern of concepts being developed so the material makes enough sense. You might need to create several versions of outline patterns to explore complex relationships and obtain greater understanding and thinking with complex or detailed material. Your objective with note writing is reaching all of your learning and performance goals.

Review relevant study notes before each class session so you remember enough for better performance with class activities. Or else you might tend to forget too much and lack adequate memory for class. Study notes help you prepare for classroom activities such as discussion, essays and small written quizzes. Then review of study notes improves your thinking and memory. When you read something important, it's wise to remember the key concepts, subtopics and their supporting points.

Group discussion often sounds too trivial and pointless when students fail to write suitable notes about the organizing points. Students recite random points and details and neglect discussion about the most important topics with their supporting points. This shows inadequate understanding and thinking about study material. Students can learn more from discussion, but this is difficult to do without writing structure notes for analysis.

Large data collections must be organized into suitable note patterns that are essential for specific analysis and applications. Too much data is available for your thinking and applications, unless you sort and organize to reach specific goals. Likewise an effective study strategy sorts and organizes material in suitable patterns for better understanding and learning performance.

The Advance Organizer method of teaching is similar to using the three level outline for your personal studying and writing. Teaching with the Advance Organizer consists of presenting the largest concepts and topics first, and then presenting detailed supporting material for these topics. This provides the structure for efficient learning with greater understanding. When your study begins with adequate focus on the organizing structure of topics in material, you can gain better understanding, thinking and improved memory of the material.

Improve your intellectual functioning for numerous activities by using the three level outline pattern for analysis of material. Simply listing the key topics in reading and study material has a powerful effect on your quality of understanding and memory, while it maintains your focus. Likewise, when you organize your key topics first for planning writing, this has a powerful effect on organizing suitable supporting material into paragraph topics. Using the three level outline for studying and writing trains you to pay attention to the organizing structure of topics in material to reach effective levels of reading, writing and thinking.

Choosing Performance Goals

When the teacher asks," what have you learned from reading?" you need to be able to explain the important points and discuss their supporting points. Or else you might be required to write an essay for a classroom activity, explaining what you have learned from the reading material. It's important to remember the key points and an evaluation of their supporting points.

Tell other people about what you have learned from reading, and discuss the most important points, presenting your opinions about the pros and cons of the material. The easiest way to achieve these goals is by writing notes about the key points and their supporting points for the central topic, so you can easily review and discuss all the important points.

Your best quality of study begins with clarifying performance goals, so you can choose suitable note patterns to reach your goals. Comprehensive analysis is important for advanced study, and complex material may require several kinds of note patterns to reach various kinds of thinking and performance goals.

School Performance Goals

Reciting - explaining key concepts and topics from reading

Discussion - about your evaluation of the central concept and the key topics along with their supporting points

Testing - with written papers and essays and various tests

Students often focus on performing well with school testing, so they can achieve their preferred level or quality of grades. School testing might consist of written essays, answers to questions, multiple choice, fill in the blanks, applying formulas or even reciting. When you know what kinds of testing you might expect, you can choose suitable note writing to prepare.

Essay tests require comprehensive analysis of study material, so these tests generally require outlines of three or more levels. Place your focus on key concepts and topics most likely to be used for essays. Your outline notes for comprehensive analysis also provide an effective means of remembering more material for the other forms of testing, such as reciting or writing answers to questions. Write lists of vocabulary terms to review for tests with items like fill-in-the-blanks or multiple choice, since these tests focus on terms such as names, places and dates.

Review your study notes before classes requiring discussion or writing an essay to show your thinking about the material. Notes for comprehensive analysis and higher levels of thinking provide preparation for advanced learning activities.

Learning with HDTV and Lists

We can expect frequent changes with our developing technology, so we must learn to use new complex equipment or procedures. Often we are getting updated versions of our computers and cell phones and other equipment. Also employees in the workplace are being retrained with updated equipment and procedures.

New technology or procedures can be found in many places, such as schools, banks, libraries and even inside our vehicles. We must learn to deal with these changes easily enough in order to take advantage of the benefits of new technology for higher level functioning. Our future is brighter with new technology, but we need efficient procedures for learning to use new complex equipment and procedures.

Employers complain that it's too difficult to train workers to use complex new equipment and procedures in the workplace. They need to provide classes and then watch over their workers to make sure they are using new machines and performing the procedures correctly to achieve work goals. Employers tend to look for workers with related education and experience, but new technology makes it too difficult to find experienced workers. The result is that employers complain about lack of suitable job applicants and that it's too expensive to train workers.

Low cost and effective training procedures are available for new employees and for retraining current employees to deal with various kinds of new equipment or procedures in the workplace. Efficient procedures are available for training employees, and these procedures can be used at home. There is no good excuse that low cost and effective training cannot be provided for the new technology changes that will continue in our future.

HDTV classes and organized lists of information are efficient methods for easily learning many complex technical activities. Instead of using teachers for each group of students, use a large screen TV to explain material and demonstrate new equipment. Very complex material can be taught with HDTV screens that show details of equipment precisely while explaining material. HDTV instruction enables students to see the presentation many times until they are certain of understanding complex material. Also provide lists of instructions for workers until they can learn to remember the steps used for complex procedures.

Organize lists of practical steps or procedures for workers, or else they can make their own lists from TV or books to learn about their new activities in the workplace. Concise and well organized lists can help workers keep track of the information and the work steps required to perform new complex activities. Eventually workers remember the procedures, or else a list can be posted by their work station to make sure that workers can keep track of new information and the steps required to perform complex technical activities in the modern workplace.

Use these learning techniques in schools, at home and work. Schools at all levels can use TV programs for teaching complex technical material, and they can use written lists for memory of specific computer activities. At work you can learn from HDTV and also write lists of new procedures. At home you can make written lists of practical steps from the instruction books of new equipment to help with learning about new complex equipment. You only need to make lists for specific applications of interest, and if you rarely use the new equipment, then you can continue using the lists to aid your memory.

THINKING STEPS

Evaluate, Synthesize, Apply

Simple reading often fails to promote sufficient thinking for the higher levels of learning, so we must learn to write suitable note patterns that help us perform various kinds of thinking activities. When you first learn to read, your goals are learning to say the words, and learning to recognize more words. Understanding the material is easy, since you're only reading very simple stories. Then as you advance through the educational levels, reading material becomes more complex so you must learn how to get greater meaning and usefulness from complex material.

Six levels of thinking indicate lower and higher level analysis. You can write summary notes to improve upon your general orientation and to improve your memory of key concepts. You can write additional notes for specific thinking goals by applying the higher levels of outlining, evaluation, synthesis and looking for the applications. Generally, you reach higher level thinking by writing more note patterns, using more study techniques and taking more time for mentally processing material.

Critical thinking skills begin with note writing for reasonably comprehensive analysis. You need to see the levels of topics and their supporting points. Then you may evaluate and synthesize material. This is usually required for advanced thinking activities. Higher level thinking is important for written essays, research papers and better quality discussion. Otherwise you might simply be dissatisfied with your learning, and wish to explore additional meaning with the material.

Meet your most challenging learning requirements by writing notes for higher levels of analysis and evaluation with material. However this requires more time, so it's not done routinely or when it's unnecessary for your goals. General analysis begins with your summary notes to organize the key concepts and their supporting points. Higher level analysis requires writing more note patterns that help you evaluate and synthesize the material, since this improves thinking for advanced functioning.

Significantly increase your understanding and memory with note writing for the higher levels of thinking. The comprehensive level of analysis requires note writing to evaluate the supporting points before you can reorganize or synthesize the material to promote ideas for problem solving. Note writing for evaluation and the practical applications of material helps you build upon critical thinking required for better performance with written essays and with many advanced learning activities.

Students tend to assume they are dumb if they must write more notes and restudy their material, but that's exactly what's required to reach greater levels of understanding and memory. Many students are only using note writing in simple ways for learning, but they should also be using note writing to improve their critical thinking skills with reading material. When students must write essays and participate in advanced quality discussion, they can perform much better with these activities if they write notes for the higher levels of analysis and evaluation.

Avoid worrying excessively about your quality of note writing, since all variations of note writing can promote better thinking. Notes can help identify key concepts, explore supporting points for topics of interest and examine complex material for greater understanding. Organizing various forms of note patterns for advanced thinking greatly improves your learning performance. Then with time and experience, the quality of your note writing and thinking continues to improve.

Several advanced study strategies are available to help you apply higher levels of analysis and thinking. All these strategies depend on note writing to help apply the higher thinking skills, and these strategies indicate that different kinds of note patterns are more effective for different kinds of material and different kinds of thinking. You can see a description of these advanced study strategies in the section below entitled "Comparing Study Strategies". Three of these advanced study strategies are called Cyber Learning, Analytical Reading and System Dynamics.

Evaluation Begins With Analysis

A remedial teacher said that her students couldn't learn well because "nothing went with anything else. Everything was mixed up all higgledy-piggledy in their heads". In other words, her students didn't understand enough about the organization and relationships in their study material. Furthermore her students were lacking good strategies for study, especially for the primary level of analysis, so they were failing to see the structure of key topics and supporting points in reading material.

Mental chaos is created by poorly organized information the same way that functional chaos is created by poorly organized materials in your home. If you have a large pile of books on the floor and wonder what you can read about a specific subject, then it's very difficult each time you choose reading material. However if your books are organized to show at a glance what titles you have for each category of subject matter, then it's easy to select from your options. Likewise, you need to see the structure of topics and supporting points in reading material for your best quality thinking.

Evaluation of material begins with an outline of key topics and their supporting points. Begin by evaluating pros and cons of supporting points for the central concept and these are the subtopics. Then evaluate supporting points that are presented for the subtopics and this is often shown with paragraph topics. Also, you might want to evaluate the usefulness and the quality of detailed material that's presented to support the paragraph topics, especially for complex technical material.

Complex material requires greater effort with note writing to reach higher levels of analysis and higher levels of evaluation. Also, you need to allow more time in your schedule, and use more note patterns to examine complex material and reach the quality of thinking required for your specific performance goals. You will find that note writing is the most efficient tool for many variations of thinking activities with complex material.

Avoid simply accepting or believing whatever you might read without evaluating it. Also avoid simply accepting whatever you hear. You need to consider any personal bias in written and spoken material and consider the limitations with some forms of knowledge. Although you may not be ready to evaluate material written by experts, at least you can weigh the pros and cons of supporting points and consider the suitability of reading material for your specific applications of interest.

Collect your own thinking notes with analysis and evaluation. Analysis requires organizing specific units of material to explore the key points. Evaluation requires weighing the pros and cons of supporting points to assess the quality of points being made. Note writing for analysis helps you evaluate material for thinking and problem solving. Analysis and evaluation of study material is essential for the higher levels of learning and thinking.

Synthesis Improves Application
Synthesize material by reorganizing and combining it with more material to grow your understanding for additional applications. Begin by outlining the structure of topics and supporting points before reorganizing and combining notes with more material to develop thinking. Study material is often somewhere along the route to becoming better developed and organized, so it may lack development for specific topics of interest. When reading material lacks coverage of topics you want to explore, reorganize and synthesize or combine it with relevant material to improve upon your knowledge for applications.

Important points might seem "hidden" in your study material because of the complexity of organizing very large quantities of material. Key topics might have been used as supporting points when they should have been emphasized as primary topics for the central concept. Reorganize your notes to place these points more prominently and synthesize these points with additional material. Otherwise you might reorganize material to simply explore some concepts and topics more sully. Evaluation and synthesis of study material promotes greater understanding of the material and helps you achieve more functioning goals.

Scientific researchers apply analysis, evaluation and synthesis to process large quantities of material for their problem solving. They begin with a problem, then collect current and relevant information about the problem. They must combine material from numerous resources, and also analyze and reorganize the material, using note patterns that promote thinking for their research goals. This activity is similar to the higher level writing projects for advanced study. Research skills require analysis and synthesis to formulate new thinking about problems.

Sometimes it's difficult to find all the worthwhile applications of study material when it has been organized in confusing ways. Although everything you read or write is organized in some form, often it's not organized in the best arrangement for your interests and applications. Reorganize poorly organized material into meaningful arrangements, so you can evaluate the quality of material for your own unique interests and applications. Also you might combine or synthesize notes with additional material to explore more ideas and useful applications.

You can uncover more applications of material by note writing to evaluate the supporting material for your topics of interest. Use suitable note writing to organize reading material according to your specific interests and your practical performance goals. Then reorganize and combine material about various topics of interest, so you can evaluate the quality of supporting material and develop suitable practical applications in terms of your specific requirements or functioning goals.

Unless you write notes to analyze, evaluate and synthesize reading material, you might find it difficult to adequately process material for greater critical thinking and practical applications. Begin with analysis and evaluation for good orientation, and add reorganization and synthesis of material to develop more ideas for problem solving and new applications.

Critical thinking begins with writing outline notes for analysis, so you can evaluate the levels of supporting points. Analysis requires taking apart the individual units of material to increase understanding, and synthesis requires putting together units of material in new ways for additional thinking. This promotes more problem solving and applications so you can achieve higher levels of thinking and functioning.

NOTES ARE THINKING TOOLS

Collecting Notes During Reading

Often you need to collect summary notes during your reading. For example if you're reading a novel, you must keep track of the characters, plots and subplots with notes during reading, or you won't remember enough to write a comprehensive summary at the end of the story. If you don't summarize the whole story adequately, it won't make enough sense. You tend to remember only random details of information, so you won't reach adequate understanding of the whole story.

Summarizing during reading is usually an efficient method of collecting notes. Summarize after every paragraph or every few paragraphs, and then after each section and chapter. If you can't find a sentence or phrase that summarizes each paragraph, write your own phrase in the margin. Otherwise simply underline summary phrases and place key words in the margin to label the key points or topics. Your key words or labels can help to review and think more effectively about the material.

Note writing is an important tool for better thinking. It's difficult to recite an explanation about any chapter unless you have written a structural summary of topics. It's difficult to write essays and discuss study material unless you organize supporting points for the key topics. It's difficult to evaluate your study material unless you analyze supporting material for the concepts and topics. Note writing helps you organize and analyze material for greater understanding and memory, and notes help you review important concepts and topics so you can continue developing your thinking about them.

You might find nuggets of wisdom in your reading material that you want to review and remember, in addition to your notes for a summary. Underline these nuggets, and list page numbers along with key words so you can find them later. Also, you might want to write notes to evaluate these nuggets so you can build upon them for your written essays.

Common Note Patterns for Study

Listed below are common organizational patterns used for study notes, but you can create your own versions and combinations of patterns according to your specific goals with study material. Summaries, outlines and diagrams are effective note patterns for common forms of analysis, but many other variations of note patterns may work better for additional thinking. You might need several kinds of note patterns for higher forms of analysis.

CATEGORIES OF NOTE PATTERNS

Lists: key points or concepts, numbered lists, pros and cons, cause and effect, series or chain of events, comparison and contrast columns, vertical or horizontal continuums, time lines

Outlines: Summaries, partial or comprehensive outlines that show the levels of topics and their supporting points

Concept Maps: concept trees, matrices, matrix comparison-contrast, column hierarchies, network hierarchies, spider maps, story maps, Venn organizers with overlapping circles

Graphs and Charts: organization charts, process or flow charts, step and process charts, linear flow charts, statistical graphs and computer programming flow charts

Diagrams: herringbone and sentence diagrams, mathematical models, engineering diagrams, operations research models and concept flow charts

Technical subject matter, such as engineering and computer programming are studied better with patterns such as concept maps and diagrams to analyze relationships in detailed material. Whereas non-technical subject matter is commonly studied with outline and summary patterns to show the levels of organizing topics. For combinations of technical and non-technical subject matter, you might need several kinds of note patterns to analyze material sufficiently for adequate understanding.

Generally begin with simple lists and outlines, then add note patterns in terms of your performance goals. It's important to realize the limitations of simply underlining notes in your book. We have all seen used textbooks with underlining that doesn't make enough sense because it looks like some random choices. Underlined notes often look mixed up when students are trying to do different kinds of thinking with one set of notes. Often it looks like students don't realize the value of organizing subtopics and supporting points before organizing other thinking notes.

Variations of Reading Notes

Study notes solve similar problems like practical notes, but for study you must sort and organize material for good performance with thinking and learning activities. On the other hand, if you're simply reading for practical applications, only organize material that you want to remember to apply. Generally, you can arrange material into different kinds of patterns that help with reaching specific goals for thinking and applications.

Different kinds of note patterns have been found to be more effective for processing different kinds of material, so note patterns can be adapted to function well for specific activities. Don't assume that one note pattern works equally well for all kinds of functioning requirements. Whether it's for thinking or practical goals, choose suitable note patterns that help you learn better with these variations of reading material.

VARIATIONS OF READING

Simple or elementary – reading for simple understanding of what's been written without preparing for any specific activities. May write casual notes about material of interest.

Skimming or speed – browsing for an orientation to general concept or seeking answers to specific questions for research. Select only information that you want to collect for your goals and applications.

Study or analytical – comprehensive analysis of material with a summary or three or four level outline as required for good understanding and performance with activities.

Research or topical – skimming for topics of interest, followed by careful reading of selected topics, then organizing notes to prepare your own topic outline for a written paper.

Technical or scientific –use note patterns like diagrams, concept maps and flow charts that help you explore the complex patterns of relationships found in highly detailed material.

Mathematical – notes may show series of steps used to solve numerical problems. Diagrams or patterns to display the correct sequence of steps. Review the steps and practice the procedures to improve your understanding and memory.

History – a time line is the most helpful note pattern to keep track of multiple events with dates. Use additional note patterns for organizing and analyzing the remaining material.

Languages – lists are typical note patterns used for memorizing vocabulary and parts of speech. Create meaningful patterns with lists that help your memory.

Novels or stories – use story-mapping diagrams to identify plots, subplots and overlapping characters among the plots. collect notes to write a comprehensive summary of the plots.

Reading, Writing and Thinking Notes

Reading without note writing is often lazy, ineffective reading. Your success with higher level education and work requires note writing for reasonably effective reading, writing and thinking. Note writing helps you pay attention to the important topics and their supporting points. It keeps your focus on the organization and summary of material. Note writing helps you organize material for the thinking activities required to reach performance goals, and it improves preparation for many kinds of activities such as reciting, discussion, writing essays and research papers. You will find that using different kinds of note patterns works better for different kinds of material and thinking activities.

Learning requirements for a course of study are expressed in terms of assignments and performance standards for grading. Generally it's wise to prepare for reciting about study material, discussion, writing essays and testing in class. Also it's wise to prepare for various kinds of writing assignments, and this might include essays in class or writing a longer paper about one of the reading topics. The quality of your writing begins with analysis of your reading material that promotes sufficient understanding for critical thinking and for adequate memory of the topics.

High school and college courses generally provide a syllabus or course outline describing the study content and assignments. Also teachers provide verbal orientation on the first day of class, so you can collect notes to supplement the syllabus with details about the learning goals and standards for grading. Survey the course requirements and choose note patterns to prepare for your specific assignments and classroom activities. Your syllabus and classroom orientation notes should help you choose suitable note patterns for your learning goals. Higher level study often requires note writing for the following kinds of activities:

Notes for High School and College Study

* Reading analysis notes to improve your thinking and memory for learning and testing goals

* Lecture notes from the teacher's presentation of material

* Thinking notes for evaluation and synthesis of study material

* Writing plan notes to prepare for written essays and reports about your reading material

* Speaking notes to present verbal reports about the subject

* Research reading notes to organize material about a specific topic for a written paper

21

Your best quality of learning during high school and college depends on suitable note writing for all of the above activities. Your knowledge content is gained from reading and classroom lectures, so it's helpful to write notes for greater learning from these activities. Your occasions for speaking and writing require planning notes for excellent performance. When you're finished with education, you should have excellent reading, writing and thinking skills, along with some worthwhile knowledge.

The value of note writing is evident when studying complex technical material. You need to see patterns of material that improve your understanding of the complex interrelationships. For engineering and math problems containing highly detailed material, several levels of diagramming might be necessary to analyze these complex interrelationships. First diagram larger patterns of relationships, and these kinds of note patterns are called concept maps or flow charts for computer programming. Then diagram separate areas of problems, adding various levels of mapping to analyze complex detailed relationships.

Social science material generally requires greater emphasis on large points. It's important to organize the largest topics or concepts into a summary, since this provides meaningful context for detailed material. For example if you're studying medicine, it's important to understand the key concepts or else the details can't be applied correctly. On the other hand, if you want to study complex machinery or rocket science it's more important to focus upon the interaction of detailed relationships or else the machinery won't work properly.

Higher levels of learning require note patterns for analyzing, evaluating and synthesizing material to promote critical thinking. You need to apply higher level thinking for problem solving and for practical applications, so you can write essays and research papers about topics of interest with good quality performance that meets your learning and functioning goals.

Notes for Practical Applications
Practical material may lack good organization for the application, so you must write notes to reorganize the material into patterns for more efficient functioning. Sort and select only the material you want to meet your specific functioning goals, and create an arrangement that's convenient for your applications. Organizing patterns like outlines, lists and charts can help you work more efficiently with some large collections of information, since these arrangements are meaningful at a glance.

Sometimes you must combine material from many different sources. Partial information may be found in many books, but you can't find adequate practical information in only one book.

For example if you're planning financial investments, often you need to gather information from numerous sources and organize note patterns for specific applications. Sort and organize only the information you want to apply. First summarize information that you gather for practical needs, and then organize into suitable arrangements for applying the material efficiently.

Improve your favorite reference resources by writing notes inside these books. Since you're sorting the material for specific goals anyway, add your notes into reference books that you may be using frequently. You can write a summary inside the front cover and mark the most important points on the pages listed. This kind of notation provides an efficient means of reviewing the material. Instead of reviewing your study notes separately, use the actual book that also contains your notes.

Add organizing information into books you're using frequently to increase their practical effectiveness. When your books lack subtitles, they can be improved by adding more levels of titles. Otherwise simply highlight or underline important points, and mark the supporting points in different colors. Add labels in the margins to identify the important points. Create higher levels of organization like an outline inside books that are lacking this quality, thereby making your most important reference books easier to use for continuous review and application.

Often recipes are written with the ingredients disorganized, so you must arrange them into the correct order for combining the ingredients. Then you must repeat this procedure every time you use the recipe, so it's easier to rewrite your recipes into the correct order you need for combining the ingredients. Likewise diet and health books are often written with recommendations disorganized and scattered throughout the book. It's impossible to apply the strategy effectively unless you reorganize the information for your practical applications.

Collect notes during casual reading to create a summary of worthwhile material. You might add large sticky notes inside the front cover to collect lists of key points along with their page numbers for easy reference about these points. Also you might underline material on the pages listed for your easy review. Always write a summary for better memory of the key concepts. Below is a useful pattern for casual reading notes.

Steps for Casual Reading Notes
Summary of strategy-organizing the topics or strategies into patterns for easy review and application

List of key points-underlining the important points and listing page numbers and key words for these points

STEPS FOR BETTER MEMORY

Review Improves Memory
It's important to review study notes right before class time, so you're prepared for classroom discussion, written essays and even a brief quiz or test. You need to improve performance in these classroom learning activities to earn higher level grades. Begin with review for greater understanding and thinking about study material, since this helps to improve your performance with writing and discussion. Then it's important to review study notes right before each specific class meets, so your memory is adequate for good performance with class learning activities so you can achieve higher quality learning and grades.

The value of review shows in your casual reading. When you read a book or article that's important to you, and never look at that material again, you tend to forget easily. Whereas if you review and think about study material occasionally, it tends to stay in your mind and even grow into more complex understanding. Reaching higher levels of learning with study material requires this kind of occasional review and thinking about material that's important for your long-term interests. Your best quality of learning always begins with note writing that facilitates better quality review and thinking.

When you remember a reasonable amount of study material, your knowledge continues to be used for thinking, for discussion, for telling others, for practical applications and for connections with future learning. Note writing begins the process of learning efficiently, but continued review is essential for very important or difficult material. Reread, resort and review study material until you remember the most important concepts. If you can't recite the concepts and key points from memory, then you're left with too little knowledge to continue learning well and thinking about the subject matter.

Reviewing and reciting are good methods for memorization, because they place your emphasis upon thinking and analysis rather than on simple forms of memorization. Adequate review of material helps you continue thinking, analyzing and building understanding. It helps you apply advanced levels of thinking to study the relationships fully. It reinforces your memory for the material you want to remember. Discussion and telling others about what you have learned is another form of review that's called reciting. Even taking a test and writing an essay provide additional forms of review.

Key Words are Memory Links

After watching the news on TV, tell someone a summary of each news story. Only very few people will remember enough to summarize all of the stories. Try watching with pen and paper, and choose one key word to represent each story. At the end of the news, make a sentence with your key words. Now you can recite a summary of all the stories easily, and even after some time has passed if you review your sentence occasionally.

Key words are a powerful memorization technique that you can adapt for many forms of study material. A key word is easier to remember than a phrase or sentence. You can label each large or small point with one key word or term. Group key words into sentences, then into stories to memorize large quantities of information if that's necessary for your goals.

Write key words in the margins during reading to represent the important points you have underlined. This helps you review and remember these points. If you don't see a logical key word, then choose a memorable term as a key word that represents the larger concept or quantity of information.

The primary memory techniques consist of organizing notes about the levels of topics, using key words, then reviewing and reciting study material several times to increase your memory. When you keep track of the organizing structure in material, this improves your understanding and memory for detailed material. Most students can remember enough for class learning activities with the review of their study notes and key words.

Study material is easily forgotten if you only read once and you don't review. If you occasionally review what you want to learn and retain, it works like magic to stay in your memory and grow more meaningful with continued thinking about the material. Review increases your understanding too, because concepts are developed slowly and the study concepts continue developing over time. Review is essential for excellent learning, and also for continued learning with material that's important for your long-term interests.

Several important learning goals are promoted by review. Note writing begins your connections for greater understanding, and then your review of material helps you continue to grow more connections for greater understanding. Review builds and reinforces your understanding and memory. It maintains good orientation for adding more material, and it helps you continue with long-term thinking so you can develop your own concepts and perspective about the topic. How often you should review or restudy depends on the complexity of the study material and on how thoroughly you want to learn.

Connections for Greater Learning
Two kinds of connections are important for learning, and both of these connections are increased by writing study notes.

Internal connections are formed when you can see the organizing points and relationships in reading material, since this helps you understand and remember more of the material.

External connections are formed when you can connect current study material with your past and future learning, so your understanding grows about the subject matter.

You can remember more by reviewing past study material occasionally. Save study materials and notes from each course of study for your future review. Save notes from your reading and research, from class lectures, discussions and also from your own thinking so study notes can be used for future review. This will improve your thinking and memory about this material.

Write key words or phrases in the margins of your notes so you can use these labels for quick review. Also you can combine notes where they are related or similar, and you can add material about the topics from other sources. For handwriting that's difficult to read for review, try small printing to create more readable notes, or else enter your notes into computer word files so you can print out neat copies that are easier to skim for your occasional review.

Note writing improves your quality of review, so you can add current learning into past and future learning to reach greater understanding about material. For example when you watch a movie that you like, you will tend to forget it soon. If you watch that movie again one or two times, you will tend to notice things that you didn't notice before and you will remember it better. Notes help with using your textbook more efficiently for review, and the review helps to maintain your memory connections so you can integrate both past and future learning.

Writing study notes helps you build more complex internal connections so you're analyzing and noticing more relationships. Exploring internal connections helps you with building greater understanding. Reviewing study notes helps you continue with building more internal and external connections. As you build more of these connections, your understanding and memory grows about the subject matter. However it's difficult to grow both of these kinds of connections unless you're writing suitable thinking notes and reviewing them occasionally.

COMPARING STUDY STRATEGIES

Common Strategies in Study Guides
The following strategies are commonly found in study guides for higher education:

Basic Study Strategies
Reading and rereading
Underlining and highlighting
3R and SQ3R study steps
Writing organized note patterns

Advanced Study Strategies
Cyber Learning by Adam Robinson
System Dynamics by Jay Forrester
Analytical Reading by Mortimer Adler

Basic Study Steps: the 3R's
The 3R sequences of study steps are activities that can improve your quality of learning. They work better if you're using a variety of procedures from different versions of 3R strategies. Many variations of 3R sequences are listed in the chart below. The basic 3R system is Read, Record and Recite. Record has been described as writing study notes based upon what you remember after reading, and Recite has been described as talking about what you remember from reading.

The 6R system consists of Reconnoiter, Read, Record, Recite, Review and Reflect. The term Reconnoiter is defined as doing a preliminary survey for an orientation before reading, and Reflect is defined as thinking about your reading material.

The most popular 3R sequence found in study guides is the SQ3R system of Survey, Question, Read, Recite, and Review. The Survey and Question steps provide your orientation for thoughtful reading, and the remaining steps consist of the common understanding of reading, reciting and reviewing.

The largest 3R sequence of study steps is OK5R, and this consists of Overview, Key ideas, Read, Record, Recite, Review and Reflect. Another related sequence is PLAN or Preview, Locate, Add and Note. In this sequence Add means including information from past learning into your current learning, and Locate means finding answers to the questions you have formed in the Preview step. Note means writing your choice of study notes about the reading material.

3R Study Steps Comparison

3R   Read, Record, Recite

SQ3R   Survey, Question, Read, Recite, Review

PQRST   Preview, Question, Read, Summarize, Test

6R   Reconnoiter, Read, Record, Recite, Review, Reflect

OK5R   Overview, Key Ideas, Read, Record, Recite, Review, Reflect

These steps fall into three categories of activities: 1) preview activities 2) reading and writing notes 3) follow-up review activities. Preview activities consist of surveying reading material and looking for the key points and forming your own questions. The second category of procedures consists of reading and recording notes, but these systems lack excellent strategies for note writing. The last category is reviewing, reciting, self testing and thinking about study material. These follow-up steps work much better if you have written adequate study notes first.

All of these 3R steps can improve your quality of study, and some steps can be omitted or done faster if your time is limited. The most important study step is writing excellent notes that help you perform better quality thinking and follow-up activities such as reviewing, reciting, testing and writing assignments.

Basic study is done with reading and writing notes for review, and the other steps may be added according to your time and goals. Most likely you will find these steps are inadequate unless you're writing study notes that help you apply suitable levels of analysis and thinking in terms of your performance goals.

Ten Styles of Learning
It has been observed that people prefer different approaches to learning. Ten different styles of learning have been identified, and five of these styles correspond to an almost opposite style of learning as shown in the following list:

Auditory versus Visual Learning. Hearing spoken words as compared to reading words or seeing pictures or demonstrations

Spatial versus Verbal Learning. Seeing arrangements of written information compared to hearing spoken information

Social versus Independent Learning. Learning in a group with others compared to studying alone

Applied versus Conceptual Learning. Performing some practical activities to learn, compared to learning by reading and thinking about ideas and information

Creative versus Pragmatic Learning. Learning by exploratory and experimental methods compared to learning by procedural and routine study methods

Technical versus Non-technical Learning

Two learning styles not listed above stand out the most in our everyday experience. These styles are called the "details person" or the technical learner versus the "main point's person" or the non-technical learner.

The "detail's person" tends to learn best by organizing details in arrangements that are both meaningful for understanding and using detailed information. The "main point's person" tends to learn best by organizing large points first, then organizing details as necessary for goals. The details learning style works better for technical subject matter where your most effective focus must be on the relationships within detailed material. The main-points style of learning works better for social sciences where large concepts provide context for detailed material.

Different note patterns are useful for these learning styles. Technical learners generally prefer diagram note patterns for examining interrelationships within complex patterns of detailed material. Whereas non-technical learners generally prefer outline patterns showing large concepts first. Understanding of technical material requires greater focus upon patterns of relationships in detailed material. Whereas understanding non-technical material requires greater focus upon the organizing concepts and topics that provide meaningful context for detailed material.

Sometimes your subject matter may contain both kinds of material, so it's better to write various kinds of note patterns and use learning strategies to deal with combinations of material effectively. You can learn more efficiently with the technical approach to learning when you're studying technical subjects. Then use the main points approach to learning when you're studying non-technical subjects. If you can identify the style of learning you prefer, focus on learning in that style. Most people cannot identify a preferred learning style, and they tend to learn best when various techniques are used for both teaching and learning. Everyone can benefit from focus upon the key topics, then studying detailed material in terms of your goals.

Three Advanced Study Strategies

Cyber Learning by Robinson recommends asking yourself twelve questions to guide reading or study, like the Socratic Method of thoughtful questioning. Then additional groups of questions are provided to build understanding, such as six journalist questions, five orientation questions and nine expert questions. In addition, ask yourself the two biggest idea-generating questions which are "What if?" and "What does this remind me of?"

This strategy also recommends organizing study notes that create mental pictures of the material, and reducing your study notes to a single sheet of material for more efficient learning. This procedure facilitates thinking and learning, but it provides limited strategy for dealing with different kinds of material.

System Dynamics is another advanced study strategy that uses note patterns to picture information. This strategy uses diagramming to essentially analyze complex interrelationships in technical material. Large "systems" can be mapped indefinitely to show how the various activities in life are connected into large and interacting systems. Separate diagrams are used to show detailed areas of the various parts of large systems. This study strategy was created by MIT professor Jay Forrester, and it's used for studying scientific material and technical engineering problems, but it's also being promoted as a learning strategy with much broader applications (Senge 231).

Diagramming and concept mapping are the preferred note patterns of System Dynamics, showing patterns of relationships in detailed technical material. These note patterns tend to be commonly used for studying engineering, complex mathematics and large systems that are "dynamic" since they are interacting and changing. Therefore the term System Dynamics is used to map and analyze complex problems of engineering systems for the practical solutions in various branches of engineering.

Study guides about this learning strategy tend to be oriented towards the applications of advanced engineering students and professional workers who deal with problems that can best be analyzed as detailed technical systems. These problems usually require dealing with very complex mathematical equations, and computer programming is generally used to calculate complex mathematical relationships that are found in large engineering systems and scientific problems.

Analytical Reading is a longstanding popular study strategy for the college level that appears to work better for studying social sciences. See the steps for Analytical Reading in "How to Read a Book" by Adler and Van Doren. Begin with the summary on page 163, and write additional summary notes about the procedures you want to focus on for learning.

The procedures for Analytical Reading can be summarized with the following three sequences of steps. The first sequence of procedures for Analytical Reading consists of classifying and summarizing the theme or unity of the book, and this provides your general orientation about the concept or topic.

The second sequence consists of outlining a book's contents, and this requires listing the major parts of a book in their order and relationships. You must understand the organization of parts in order to understand the whole book comprehensively. Also, identify the problems that the author is trying to solve. Identify the key terminology the author is using, identify the leading propositions and arguments, and finally identify if the author has solved the problems posed by the book. Use these steps in reverse order for planning writing. The reader should try to uncover the book's structure with an outline, while the writer must create structure with an outline in order to present an organized message and theme in a written paper.

A third sequence of study activities consists of three steps for evaluating the book. Your first step is judging if the author is uninformed or misinformed. The second step is judging if the author's work is incomplete or illogical, and finally present good quality reasoning for all of your opinions and evaluations. You can perform all of these steps much better with written notes that help you keep track of your thinking about the material.

The guide to Analytical Reading also includes procedures for research called "syntopical reading". This specialized form of reading is defined as exploring one topic by sorting numerous information resources. First, read by skimming to locate the kind of material you want about your topic in each resource. Then carefully read the material about your chosen topic to select information that meets your inquiry goals, taking notes.

Additional steps are provided for syntopical reading. The first sequence of steps consists of inspecting the books, identifying the terminology and clarifying the questions you're exploring. The next two steps consist of defining your issues and analyzing discussions in books that you have selected. These are basic fundamental steps for research, but it's important to realize these steps also depend upon suitable note writing.

These advanced study strategies vary in efficiency depending on your material and goals. The note patterns of Cyber Learning work like summary notes with questions to stimulate thinking. The diagrams of System Dynamics work better than outlines to improve upon your analysis of technical material. The outline for Analytical Reading is valuable, but it lacks focus on evaluating supporting points for all levels of topics, then using this kind of structure to organize good quality writing.

Your Future Learning
Learning goes on indefinitely as long as you continue reading, writing and thinking. Your best quality of mental growth requires using all of the techniques for learning described in the steps for teaching. It requires reading, writing, speaking and also thinking about your study material. When some of these activities are neglected, your quality of learning is diminished. Furthermore, you can significantly improve your learning skills by processing reading material with suitable note writing for the higher levels of analysis and thinking.

You can increase your learning with strategies like rereading and restudying. When you reread previous study material after some time has passed and write new notes, you may find that your understanding has grown and changed, especially for complex material. Apply this process occasionally to "grow your thinking when you're seeking to increase your level of learning. Your intellectual growth results from new connections that you're forming by continued thinking about material, and this process helps you build higher levels of learning.

Professional occupations require expert levels of learning in the subject matter, and you can achieve expert level learning by applying effective study procedures over a long period of time. Professional workers such as doctors and lawyers must rely upon organized information and efficient techniques to process large quantities of material. Also this is useful for the average person who wants to become better informed. The best strategies for learning more efficiently are seeking better organized materials and writing suitable notes for analysis to process study material for better thinking and memory.

Too much information is available to read or study everything you might want to learn. But you can learn more by using highly organized information and by organizing notes for greater levels of analysis to achieve your learning and functioning goals. Build more internal learning connections by studying with note writing, then occasionally review your material so you continue growing your understanding and building external learning connections. Although you probably won't be able to learn as much as you want, you can specialize or focus on learning in subject matter that's most important for your long-term interests.

Today we have greater access to information for learning, but many resources are lacking good organization. Therefore it takes too much time and effort to process the information for good understanding and applications. The solution consists of seeking information resources that are better organized, and using more efficient procedures for processing information.

Computer word processing makes it easier to organize and reorganize information collections and create more note versions for thinking and applications. Collecting study notes in computer word-processing programs is a very efficient means of improving your productivity with processing information.

Our brains are similar to computers and require organization and labels to store and recall large quantities of information. Information is organized in computers with address labels used for memory paths to storage locations. Our brains can benefit from writing notes that help identify the organization of topics, while key words work as labels to link our memory to larger quantities of information. However the advantage of our brains over computers is that we can add our own ideas and reorganize information into more meaningful patterns that can grow our understanding. Therefore we learn more by organizing notes for the various forms of analysis with material.

Our future learning is greatly enhanced by new technology. The computer, the internet and new HDTV are tools with great potential to provide easy and low cost learning for everyone around the globe. Instead of paper books, we can read endless quantities of e-books with computers. We can take any classes with television, learning from "easy-to-see" demonstrations of complex procedures that can be played over again many times. We can save our own ideas and gain endless access to sharing information and ideas with others on the internet.

Reading a Chapter Every Day
Everyone enjoys some casual reading, but consider setting goals for some additional learning instead of reading only randomly. Identify personal interests for general learning and research. You might prefer to gain some expertise about your favorite topics. Easily attain your goals with the habit of reading one or more chapters daily. You may be motivated to read several chapters on many days, since your reading speed and efficiency improves so greatly when you're summarizing material.

Try to form the habit of reading at least a chapter every day, or several chapters a week. It's an easy way to improve your education with your choice of material. However if you don't know about the importance of writing summaries, you might fail to obtain enough benefit from reading. Without summary notes, you might fail to learn well, forget material too easily and lack the means of reviewing material efficiently. You may end up with too little learning for your time and effort. Using good strategies such as writing summary or outline notes improves learning efficiency so that you may choose to read a larger quantity of material on a regular basis.

The following steps are fairly effective if you want to read a challenging book in only one day. Skim through the book to look for large concepts and subtopics. Decide what supporting points you want to gather about the topics of interest and take notes about the material for review. Although you won't remember all of the details, prepare a written list of key topics and supporting points that you want to review occasionally.

Reading a challenging book in one day isn't recommended for college level study. For serious learning, this study pace is called "cramming" and for good reason. When you try to learn at this pace, your mind lacks sufficient time for thinking and integrating new material with past knowledge. So the result is lower quality thinking. Better quality learning requires more time for thinking about the material. Cramming doesn't work for your best quality of study, but you might prefer this pace for leisure reading.

Choosing goals is an effective activity for learning more from leisure reading. Set goals and set out reading material, along with note paper, so it's handy for spare time reading.

"Summarize and Save" Your Best Strategies

When you find an interesting strategy, "summarize and save it" so you're collecting a variety of useful strategies. Using more study strategies provides flexibility for more efficient learning with different kinds of material and goals. Collect strategies for your other important activities too, such as researching and writing, getting organized and career planning.

The easiest way to save strategies is writing simple outlines, summaries and other note patterns to provide a shorter version. You can manage much larger quantities of information for your understanding and applications by writing a summary or other note pattern that creates a shorter version for easy review. Simply choose the largest concepts and key points, and organize them into an effective pattern for your occasional review.

People tend to forget strategies when they need them most. Although this problem is very common, it's totally unnecessary. "Summarize and save" the best strategies you find or you will tend to forget them. Then you will have an incredibly difficult struggle coping with your important activities. Keep reminders and summaries of your best strategies handy so you won't forget to apply them during important activities.

Keep your strategies handy in note books or posted nearby for a reminder where you're doing that kind of activity. You can organize your strategies by topics in notebooks and post a reminder near your study desk. Keep your favorite strategy summaries handy so you can remember to apply your best strategies when you need them.

SUMMARY

The goal of education is gaining higher level learning skills with reading, writing and thinking, besides gaining useful knowledge. Simple reading is inadequate for higher level study, because you might not notice and remember enough important points, and you won't have an efficient means of reviewing them. Note writing helps you keep track of the key concepts, the levels of topics and the supporting points. Regardless of how many study strategies you apply, if you can't say an explanation about the key points in reading material, your learning is inadequate.

List the key points or subtopics first in your study material, and organize supporting points for these subtopics. You can analyze material more fully by outlining all levels of topics with their supporting points. Choose suitable note patterns for the analysis of different kinds of material and to maintain adequate focus on your performance goals. When reading for study, you must find the structure of topics and supporting material, so you can evaluate the pros and cons of supporting points. When writing, you must create the structure of key topics with their supporting points, since this provides good development and organization of material for better quality paragraphs.

Critical thinking for higher learning begins with writing notes for analysis to evaluate supporting points for topics of interest. Writing notes for synthesis of specific topics requires that you reorganize and combine material to develop more knowledge or strategy to grow your understanding for various applications. Thinking skills require analyzing, evaluating and synthesizing material to reach the higher levels of functioning with learning. Use good writing strategy to develop your ideas and share them with others. Writing suitable notes for critical thinking about material and for planning writing is essential to develop higher level learning skills with reading, writing and thinking.

All outstanding study strategies recommend writing notes. The 3R strategy of "read, record and recite" depends upon "recording study notes". Analytical Reading begins with writing a full outline of the material, followed by examining the leading propositions and arguments for analysis. System Dynamics uses diagramming to explore patterns of interrelationships in complex detailed material. Cyber Learning recommends writing short notes in your choice of memorable patterns and using expert questions to guide higher levels of thinking. Written notes are valuable for most forms of mental activities, and your choice of note patterns can be adapted for specific material and goals.

Students in higher education should know about the various study strategies and applications for written notes so they can use flexibility in choosing the best strategies to reach their goals. Teachers should know about many study strategies and include them in assignments so students are getting adequate practice with effective learning skills. Some study techniques are optional and their usage depends upon time and learning goals. However summary notes are essential for all forms of intellectual activity, and they help with processing study material efficiently. You can learn without writing study notes, but it takes more time and effort and you might fail to achieve adequate learning.

You can learn more by using better study strategies and by restudying material. However you must be practical about time and energy, and realize that you don't have an endless amount of time for restudying material when you're a student in school. The fundamental strategy of writing suitable summary notes is sufficient to meet most study goals in the limited amount of time that's typically available for study. That's why it's so important to study with note writing, and then to budget your time with planning and distributing your workload into a time schedule. If you want to study more thoroughly for difficult courses, then take smaller workloads so you have enough time to apply more note writing strategies for greater analysis.

Note writing is essential to reach higher levels of functioning with many mental activities. The following chapter covers the numerous applications for written notes such as creating a plan for writing, planning for speaking and teaching, and writing notes from your listening and thinking activities. Written notes are both flexible and interchangeable, because similar kinds of note patterns are useful for all variations of intellectual activities. You can increase your learning and intellectual growth significantly by writing suitable notes to analyze material for study and other variations of your thinking activities.

Steps to Improve Learning

Summarize by listing subtopics and their supporting points

Outline by organizing the levels of topics and supporting points

Gain comprehensive understanding by fully outlining material

Evaluate supporting points for the levels of topics in material

Organize suitable lists or notes for specific performance goals

Review your notes for higher quality thinking and memory

Write higher level thinking notes for advanced learning

Occasionally tell others about study material and topics

Prepare to discuss your evaluation of important topics

Write variations of notes to achieve all functioning goals

Before important classroom activities, review your notes

Continue learning by reading at least a chapter a day

Use organized summaries to save important information

Use regular practice to improve learning and thinking skills

2 WRITING AND RESEARCHING

Writing Steps

PLAN by choosing your topic, subtopics and paragraph topics

WRITE discussion with your supporting material for the subtopics and paragraph topics

REVISE to improve the quality of your paragraphs and sentences

STRATEGY FOR WRITING

Students often write poor quality papers in terms of strategies for thinking and writing. These skills are important for all forms of communication activities in schools and careers, and they also depend upon note writing for analysis described in the previous chapter. Generally, students fail to include their own thinking sufficiently in written papers because they fail to write suitable notes for analyzing their reading material and planning writing. Students need better strategies for studying, critical thinking and planning writing, so they can organize material sufficiently with their own thinking when planning writing.

Three important steps for all forms of communication are listed above for planning, writing and revising your written and spoken messages

Three important skills for essays and research papers consist of: 1) organizing your reading notes for suitable levels of analysis 2) applying advanced levels of thinking to form your own views with reading material 3) using good strategy to organize your writing plan

Many students are simply writing rambling rhetoric, lacking in sufficient organization and quality of thinking, because they lack good strategies for writing. Often they simply shuffle around other people's written material. This doesn't present their own thinking about the topic and material, and the result is poor quality writing. The concept of good writing requires that you present your own thinking and perspective about the topic.

Good quality writing begins with good strategies for studying, thinking and writing. The study strategy in this guide promotes adequate analysis for the higher levels of thinking, so you can form your own opinions for writing. The writing strategy uses effective levels of organization for writing: topic, subtopics and paragraph topics. This structure makes it easy to choose your own levels of topics and present your own thinking.

Writing a long paper is too complex to do a good job with one single step. Students who write long papers in one single step get poor quality results. Any complex activity must be broken down into separate steps to focus on each stage of the activity, and the result is better quality work being done more efficiently. Three steps listed above are the key to excellent written papers. Also these steps can improve short papers and personal notes, and your papers will be much easier to write. Even if you have plenty of talent for writing, you won't get good enough results by writing long papers in one single step.

Three steps for writing focus on the difficulties in this process. Students might begin writing with step two, but at some point it's important to deal with all of these steps for excellent results. If you begin with step three, you focusing on details of sentence quality or fancy rhetorical style. This focus tends to produce elegant sentences that are deficient in adequate quality of ideas. If you begin writing with step two, you're focusing upon creative development of detailed material. Later this material must be organized around subtopics or your message is too disorganized and difficult to understand. You can expect improved results by beginning with step one for planning your structure of subtopics and paragraph topics before organizing detailed material.

Organization is the most important quality for all forms of communication and this begins with your outline to plan writing. Step one organizes your writing by listing your concept or topic, then key points or subtopics and supporting paragraph topics. Step two is the focus on explaining your paragraph material. Step three places the focus upon revising and improving your paragraphs and sentences. Additional techniques may be useful to improve upon writing, but the primary concepts for written communication are found in the following steps:

STEP ONE

Planning Writing
Often students simply begin writing their ideas, but this won't work well for long papers. Most likely you won't have enough ideas to create the length, and even short papers can present this problem. Furthermore, it's difficult to develop enough ideas and material unless you understand the concept of choosing your large points first, then organizing enough detailed material around these points to create the length. Otherwise your paper will be lacking in suitable quantity and organization of material to create the length and quality of paper you want.

Plan writing by choosing your central concept and title first. Now choose your key points or subtopics to support the concept. Then choose enough paragraph topics to support the subtopics and to create the length of paper you want. You might gather detailed material first, then choose your title, subtopics and the paragraph topics you want for supporting all of your subtopics. For short papers, simply list your subtopics to use for paragraph topics. For long papers, list enough paragraph topics to support your subtopics and to plan the length of paper.

Step one separates your thinking about the organizing topics from detailed material. It's important to list all your paragraph topics first, because it's inefficient to go back and forth between thinking about large points versus detailed material. Often it's so inefficient that it's difficult to think of any more subtopics and paragraph topics after writing some detailed material. You will find that it's more efficient to organize thinking into three steps. You will tend to get more ideas during each step, since your thinking is focused more efficiently for each activity.

Organize your current ideas and material about a topic first when planning writing. First list the concepts and title, and your largest key points for subtopics. This reveals if you have enough material in mind to write your paper with only current thinking and material. Otherwise, your planning notes provide direction for gathering more material from research reading, discussion and continued thinking. It's helpful to choose topics of personal interest so that it's easier to form your own opinions and present your personal perspective about the topic.

Show your own thinking by choosing your own title, subtopics and paragraph topics for a writing plan. After collecting material about the topic for your paper, organize suitable note patterns for analysis and for developing higher level thinking about your collection of material. Develop your own views about the topic by evaluating the pros and cons of supporting points found in collected material. Also gather discussion notes from talking with other people and add these ideas along with your thinking notes, so you can include them in your writing plan outline when you're planning the supporting material for a written paper.

Write a summary paragraph for an introduction or conclusion within your written paper. Then your reader will find it easier to understand your key concept and the subtopics provided in your message. When you have recommendations you want to place in your conclusion, then summarize in your introduction. Otherwise place your summary in the conclusion, and you could introduce your message with other techniques. You could pose questions that you want to answer, or you could introduce the central concept(s) or theme that you're exploring.

Your writing plan creates a summary for a written message. Planning should list your key concepts, title and the supporting subtopics, and then enough supporting paragraph topics for the length of paper. Outline your ideas and material at hand before collecting more material. Planning helps you organize meaningful levels of topics with your own choice of supporting material.

Outline for Planning Writing

This three level outline is equally effective for planning writing and for analyzing reading material.

Topic - title to focus concept
  Subtopics - key points about the topic
    Paragraph Topics - supporting points for subtopics

Using this three level outline for planning writing helps you solve the following problems of writing:

1) Organize enough material for the length of paper. When you list your concepts and the key points first, then you may simply list the supporting paragraph topics and organize enough detailed material to create the length of paper.

2) Present your own views and perspective on a topic. Choosing your own subtopics and paragraph topics for writing helps you organize collected material with your own perspective. Using the three level outline to evaluate reading material helps you can form your own opinions, so you can organize your own views about the topic when planning writing.

3) Develop better supporting material for paragraphs. When you outline your subtopics and their supporting points for your paragraph topics, your detailed material can be organized into better quality paragraphs.

Choose your key points first for your writing outline about the topic, and then organize supporting points and detailed material into paragraph topics. Without this kind of organizing structure, writing tends to ramble around, lacking suitable organizing points and supporting material. Using the three level outline pattern above helps you organize your thinking and material about any topic to provide clarity about what you want readers to understand about your perspective on the topic.

Writing strategies tell you to plan writing with an outline, but they don't tell you that an effective outline begins by choosing your largest points for subtopics first so you can choose suitable supporting paragraph topics. Now you can organize your own thinking and collected material within this structure, presenting your own perspective. Generally your concept for a message is supported by your key points that create the subtopics, and then you can organize suitable supporting paragraph topics.

Readers need to see organization in written material. These steps are useful to organize written and spoken communication.

Steps for Planning Writing

Topic or Concept – choose your key concept(s) or strategy and the title for a message

Subtopics – choose your key points or subtopics to support the topic. You might introduce each subtopic with a summary paragraph or else use subtitles for long papers

Paragraph Topics – list enough paragraph topics to show your supporting points for subtopics and create the length of paper

Length of Paper – estimate the number of paragraphs required for the length of paper so you can list enough paragraph topics

Outline Current Ideas and Material - about the topic before looking for additional supporting material

Introduction or Conclusion – summarize the central concept about the message for an introduction or conclusion

In summary, clarify your large concepts and choose the title. Then support this concept by choosing key points or subtopics, and list supporting paragraph topics for the length of paper. Finally, organize enough detailed material for your paragraphs, using your own ideas and collection of material about the topic. When planning writing, you must create the structure of topics to organize suitable supporting material so that your paragraphs show adequate quality focus and organization.

Planning the Length of Papers
The goal of planning writing is listing enough paragraph topics for the length of paper, while organizing your levels of topics. Generally you can list one topic for each paragraph to create the length of paper. Also add one paragraph for your introduction and/or conclusion in most papers. So how do you estimate the number of paragraphs that will fit on one page?

Generally three average-sized paragraphs will fit on one page that's typewritten and double spaced with one-inch margins all around. This estimate is similar for handwritten papers with medium-sized handwriting. For small paragraphs count two of them as one medium-sized paragraph, or else four or five small paragraphs can fit on one page.

Count the number of paragraph topics needed for the length of your written paper. For example, a three page paper contains nine paragraphs, or else eight paragraphs with an introduction or conclusion. You might list a few extra points to have handy if some paragraphs are short ones. Also, you can adjust the final length of your paper by adding or taking away some detailed material from the paragraphs.

For short papers: simply list a subtopic for each paragraph in your preferred order, since greater organization is generally unnecessary. Or else you can simply list the number of points you want for paragraph topics that create the length of paper. You probably have adequate material in mind about many topics to write short papers with current thinking. You don't need to gather material for written essays and your personal letters. Simply write whatever you think, or whatever you can create about each topic listed in your writing plan.

For long papers: choose enough key points for subtopics, so you can organize enough supporting paragraph topics to create the length of paper. Introduce each subtopic with a summary paragraph or a subtitle, or else you could simply write your paragraph topics and let readers infer what are your subtopics. Now decide if you want to look for more information, or else if you want to write this paper only with your current thinking.

Writing a personal letter illustrates the simple procedure you can use for writing short papers. Simply list the topics you want covered in your letter. Now write one or more paragraphs with your current thinking about each topic. Personal letters might contain different topics instead of creating a theme with related paragraphs like the typical school paper or essay. Also this easy approach to writing works for short school papers and essays. Simply begin by listing the paragraph topics you want to use, and then write your current thinking about each topic.

Plan essay tests by listing one topic for each paragraph you must write. First count the number of paragraphs you need to fill your essay booklet. Usually it's one paragraph per page. Now list one subtopic or point for each paragraph before writing your detailed discussion about each point.

There's no greater fear during an essay test than writing one great paragraph, and then being unable to think of more points for the other paragraphs. Most likely you have used all of your large points inside one paragraph, and you don't realize that you have summarized points that should be explained in separate detailed paragraphs. You can prevent this problem by listing all your paragraph topics first, then you can distribute your detailed material better among these paragraph topics.

Essay tests require your current thinking about the material, and this depends on your memory for the important concepts and subtopics from reading. Essays show your personal opinions and evaluation of the pros and cons of material. For essays you can only write what's currently in your mind. However if you have studied by writing suitable notes for analysis, then you will have enough material in mind to write good essays.

Plan the length of written papers by choosing subtopics first and then listing enough supporting points for paragraph topics to create the length of paper. Simple planning is listing only the number of paragraph topics you want for the length of paper, then writing your current thinking about each topic. Complex planning for long papers is choosing concept(s) and subtopics for the longer length. Then choosing enough supporting points for the paragraph topics and organizing suitable detailed material. Also it's much easier to include your own views about the topic, when you choose topics of personal interest.

Key Concepts for Writing

First choose your largest points for the message is a key concept for writing. Begin with your concepts or strategy and title for a message, and then choose your largest points for the message. Use your large points for subtopics, and use supporting points for paragraph topics. When reading, you must find the organized pattern of key concept(s), subtopics and their supporting points. When writing, you must create your own pattern of concepts, subtopics and supporting points to organize material.

Good communication requires organized levels of topics with suitable supporting material. The three-level outline pattern is useful to organize effective writing by choosing your own topic, subtopics and supporting paragraph topics. This pattern is highly effective to plan meaningful structure for writing, while it helps with organizing your own ideas and perspective.

Another key concept is the quantity of detailed material you need depends on the length of paper and the information goals for your message. For school papers, you must organize the quantity of detailed material necessary to meet the length requirements for an assigned paper. For business writing, you must present the level of detail that's necessary to meet the information goals for your message. For long school papers, choose your topic carefully so you can find or create enough detailed material for the required length of paper.

Long papers must contain substantial quantities of detailed supporting material to create the longer length. This concept is vitally important for excellent long papers. Long papers don't merely summarize topics. Short papers have more characteristics of a summary, whereas long papers require greater division of subtopics to organize more paragraphs with much greater quantities of detailed material to create the length. Use more organizing points to prepare sufficient material when planning long papers. Divide your subtopics into enough paragraph topics for long papers to organize suitable detailed material.

Long complex papers require greater concept development to organize the structure for large quantities of detailed material. You can best organize the material by using a three level outline. Clarify your concept and list your key points for the subtopics, listing their supporting points for paragraph topics. Sometimes you need to be more creative and flexible with developing your material, and simply begin writing your ideas for the important concepts. However most of the time you can get better results by planning your material with the three level outline, especially for school papers or business and professional papers.

Unusually long papers may be divided into chapters to plan each subtopic separately, although it's important to create a unified theme by choosing your largest points for each chapter first. Writing a long paper is similar to writing numerous short papers. Most likely you will be planning and writing paragraphs separately for each section or chapter. You can write one chapter of your paper, and return to the planning process to organize detailed material for the next chapter. For long papers you need to plan more levels of topics and also use subtitles to separate the sections and call attention to your key points.

Plan fiction writing by outlining your basic plot and subplots, and then choosing your cast of characters as much as possible. As you develop action scenes, you must provide suitable detailed activity and conversation to provide development of your basic plot and subplots and to reach your goal for the length of story. You can plan two levels of supporting material for fiction writing.

Briefly outline detailed material that you want for each subplot you're creating. Then plan for the quantity of detailed material you need to meet the information goals of the plots, and for the length requirements of the story.

A variety of methods are useful to gather material for long written papers, such as reading, thinking and discussion to help you grow more of your own ideas and concepts about the topic. You can read relevant materials to stimulate your thinking about the topic. Your ideas may grow like magic during reading and thinking, but you must take notes to collect and save your ideas. You may find that some topics are very easy to develop, whereas other topics require much greater effort to grow your thinking and to create discussion about specific topics you want covered in your written message.

STEP TWO

Writing Paragraphs

Write one or more paragraphs for each paragraph topic, or else subtopic for short papers. Present explanation or discussion with detailed material for each paragraph topic, weaving together the points in your writing plan with current thinking. Organize the sequence of your material for each topic to create discussion that contributes to developing the topic and theme.

Show your subtopics or key points with summary paragraphs, or else by using subtitles that call attention to these subtopics. It's important to emphasize your subtopics in written material, and then develop each topic with enough supporting material. Explain relationships formed by your unique organization of the material, and explain any new connections that you're creating with your collection of material. Keep an open mind for building upon your topic by adding more ideas and material when you develop the paragraphs, since your concepts can be expected to continue growing during the process of writing.

You might begin each paragraph with a general statement. Then add the material from your planning outline, using current thinking to create your own unique analysis and organization of material that you have gathered for a message. It's important to present your personal perspective about each paragraph topic by including your own thinking about the material you organized to support each paragraph topic.

Paragraph development should create interest in each topic and also support an integrated theme about the central concept. Written material is similar to ordinary conversation in this way. If you briefly state an interesting point, then say nothing else about it, people tend to ignore the point even if it's very good.

It's better to add detailed material and discussion to get people thinking about the significance of that point. Present a suitable quantity of discussion to support each point and also to meet the length requirements for your paper. Organize the sequence of material throughout your paper, so you're creating an integrated message with your discussion about each topic.

Open each paragraph with an interesting topic sentence that leads a reader into your specific material organized for the topic. When paragraphs begin with interesting summary sentences, it sharpens the readers' attention on the topic so they can focus better on the quality of your supporting material. Sometimes it's easier to create an adequate summary sentence after you have finished writing the paragraph. Topic sentences should provide orientation and summary, so they create an introduction for paragraphs that are easier to read and understand.

Writing is saying whatever you want to say about the topic. It's whatever explanation and material you want to present for those points you have chosen to include for a written message. You might simply begin by speaking about your ideas before writing them with reasonably good sentences and organization. Magic occurs when organizing and writing your ideas on paper. Writing your current ideas promotes additional thinking, so you can build upon ideas and material to reach greater development. You can continue building upon current material and ideas to fully develop your unique views about a topic.

Occasionally you might find yourself struggling to develop sufficient discussion about topics that you want included in your message. Stimulate your creative thinking with related reading and discussion about those topics you have chosen to include. Also you can grow more ideas by explaining the topics to others. When you express ideas verbally it tends to generate additional discussion and thinking. The topics in your writing plan are also useful for interesting discussion topics, but remember to collect interesting ideas from discussion with note writing so you can add this material into your writing plan.

Avoid simply shuffling around collected material, or it tends to look like "copied material" or plagiarism even when you're documenting all of the sources. The goal is showing your own thinking with a collection of material. You can create a unique message only by choosing your own organizing structure and paragraph topics, and then by including your own thinking. This requires note writing for the advanced levels of thinking such as analysis, evaluation and synthesis. Also this requires building an adequate writing outline so you can develop your own unique message that you want to create about the topic.

Focus on Current Thinking

Don't stop to think about sentence quality during this step, or else the quality of your ideas and thinking will be diminished. This step is an exclusive focus upon thinking and writing your ideas about each paragraph topic. All distractions that interrupt your concentration will diminish your thinking and the quality of ideas being produced for each topic. Concentrate on developing detailed discussion about each topic in your writing plan and on fully capturing your thinking about the topic.

Keep your focus on current thinking when writing paragraphs, or else ideas may escape before being developed and written. Concentrating on current thinking produces "stream of thought" writing with spontaneity and continuity that makes your writing sound like conversation, and therefore more interesting to read. It creates an interesting flow of ideas that holds a reader's attention like speech. However step one must be done first before this step can be done effectively. It's essential to choose your key points and paragraph topics first, before organizing suitable detailed material to support these points.

Writing current thinking is like catching "birds on the wing", since ideas are fleeting and elusive. Ideas are usually "passing thoughts" and quickly forgotten if you don't write them down. Typically when you get an idea that's not related to your current activities, you must write it down or you will soon forget. Avoid distractions and keep your "train of thought" going in this step. It's important to write your ideas as soon as you're thinking about them, and then continue with your thinking and writing to fully develop your ideas for each paragraph topic.

Occasionally your creativity might be stimulated by beginning writing with step two, or by simply writing your current thinking about the topics for your message. If this produces sufficient material for your goals, then simply check the organization of your material for the next step. Generally it's more efficient to begin with a writing plan to organize the theme and subtopics before choosing paragraph topics. Although it's important to begin with a writing plan, your plan may be changing, especially when writing long and complex papers. So you might want to revise your plan occasionally to include new ideas.

Sometimes a writing plan is only a good beginning, since you might continue developing and building upon your material as long as you want. Your final writing plan might look different, since you may continue revising your concepts and theme while developing your paragraph topics. So leave room for growth in your writing plan to promote development of more thinking and material within the framework started by your planning.

Organizing Paragraphs

Paragraph organization begins with a writing plan that lists your topic, your subtopics and enough supporting paragraph topics. Planning organizes your structure of key points and supporting points, so that subtopics and paragraphs support your central theme. This helps you avoid disorganized paragraphs that jump among topics and ramble around. Planning organizes material into levels of topics that create an integrated message.

Your personal subjective opinion is involved in choosing and organizing suitable paragraph topics to support a central theme. It depends upon what you choose to do with your collection of ideas and material. Nevertheless, good paragraph organization always begins with a writing plan to organize your own unique structure of subtopics and paragraph topics to create your theme about the topic. A writing plan also helps to organize your own thinking, helping you create a unique message.

Paragraphs are better organized when they begin with a topic or summary sentence. Topic sentences help to focus attention upon the central topic, before presenting detailed supporting explanation or discussion. Generally, it shouldn't be too difficult to find the topic sentences and to understand paragraph topics. Sometimes paragraphs must be organized in sequential order like story telling, and the topic sentences may be located at the end. Occasionally topic sentences may be located inside of the paragraphs. However when paragraphs are lacking in topic sentences, they are usually lacking in sufficient summary and organization for easy reading and understanding.

Short paragraphs are the trend in writing today, so your material might be distributed into lower levels of topics that contain less supporting material. Sometimes paragraphs turn out like magic to develop a very interesting point. At times paragraphs might consist of poorly related sentences. These poor quality paragraphs can be improved with an effective topic sentence at the beginning, making it easier to organize suitable material for the topic. When paragraphs contain several topics, they can be divided into separate small paragraphs.

Warm up your writing skills any time by choosing a topic and writing a paragraph. Or else you might list a subtopic and write a few paragraphs about it. Otherwise outline your leading points for any topic, adding paragraph topics for a longer essay that creates discussion about the points. Choose any topic of interest and list paragraph topics to create the length of paper you want. Now simply write current thinking about each paragraph topic. You can imagine how easy it would be to write a one-page essay with the following subtopics.

List of Subtopics for an Essay

Title: The Race Car
Paragraph 1: Car body design
Paragraph 2: Engine description
Paragraph 3: Road handling
Conclusion: A winning combination

As you can see, it looks fairly easy to write a paragraph about each topic once you have selected all of your paragraph topics. Now simply write whatever comes to your mind about each paragraph topic. You can present current thinking and create discussion with your ideas, and the only requirement is creating fairly well organized material about each paragraph topic.

If you want to write a longer paper about this topic, simply add more subtopics or divide the subtopics into more paragraph topics. Also you might add more detailed material inside your paragraphs. Examples of additional paragraph topics for this paper might be as follows: tire quality, driving conditions, racing uniforms, refueling problems and car maintenance requirements. Long papers are much easier to write when you choose topics of personal interest, so that you're organizing larger quantities of detailed material you find interesting.

STEP THREE

Revising Writing

This step is your opportunity to improve poor quality sentences and paragraphs and to check the quality of grammatical details. When you're writing quickly to capture your thinking in step two, this may result in some poor quality sentences and paragraphs. Therefore step three is essential to improve all aspects of your writing that must be ignored during your exclusive focus upon thinking and writing discussion about the paragraph topics.

Set aside your paper for awhile and return to it later with a fresh critical view of what can be improved. Return to it later during the day or several times during each day to see if you notice errors or room for improvement. Repeat this procedure as many times as necessary to improve all aspects of your writing until you're satisfied with the quality of details. You can expect to find substantial room for improvement after writing quickly about your ideas, especially for long papers. Depending upon the amount time you have, continue working on improvements until you reach the level of quality you want.

You may find yourself getting many ideas for improving both subtopics and paragraph topics while working on the details of writing quality. Check that each subtopic is logically supported with organized material. Check the quality of your paragraphs so you can improve discussion that lacks sufficient development to support the subtopic it covers. Revise inadequate development of subtopics and paragraphs if you see room for improvement in developing the quality of your message.

Strong paragraphs begin with an interesting topic sentence that catches a reader's interest. Revise paragraphs that contain only weak support for the topic and subtopic. When you outline your topic sentences under each subtopic, they should show good organization and development for your theme. Work on the quality of individual paragraphs until you're satisfied with their contribution to each subtopic. The level of development you reach depends on the amount of time you have and the level of quality you want for your written message.

Proof read your sentences to check for grammatical quality and clarity of expression. You might find awkward sentences with poor choice of wording, or else redundant expressions. Reorganize poor quality sentences to sharpen the focus and clarify the meaning. It has been said that important points tend to go unnoticed unless they are repeated a few times, but even good tactics can be overdone. This step is your opportunity to check all kinds of details inside your individual sentences and paragraphs and to correct weaknesses that would distract from the quality and meaning of your message.

Include new ideas when revising paragraphs and subtopics, since your concepts may continue growing during the process of writing. Check for adequate development of your key concept with subtopics that support your theme. Use your new ideas to build upon your central theme and create a more interesting message. Then revise or reorganize the supporting material to sharpen the paragraph focus. This step is your opportunity to improve the focus of your theme and to create an integrated message with well developed supporting material.

Word-processing programs with spell-check and grammar checking features may save time, but they won't correct all kinds of problems with your writing details. They won't deal with insufficient supporting material for paragraphs and concepts, and they won't deal with poor quality organization of sentences and supporting material. They won't deal with unnecessary words or awkward expressions in your sentences. Work on all forms of revisions that are important for developing the quality of your message. Continue with revisions as long as necessary to reach your goals for the project.

Solving Problems with Revisions

If you want good grades on written papers, leave enough time for step three so you can revise your paper until it looks like excellent quality work. The last step is your opportunity to correct all remaining defects, and this often determines the appearance and grade of a paper. Writing "last minute papers" doesn't leave enough time for the revisions of step three, so you may turn in school papers that look like poor quality even when your first two steps were an excellent beginning.

You can get better results by taking more time, so avoid writing "last minute" long papers. Occasionally doing a little work generally is more effective than one or two longer sessions. Schedule enough time to reach the higher standards required for long complex papers. These papers are long-term projects, so it might be necessary to go back and forth several times among the steps for writing. Also you might consider adding more steps or areas of focus. For the fairly inexperienced student writer, it's important to schedule enough time to get good results.

You always have time limitations for school papers, so you must manage time to reach your goals for reasonable writing in the time schedule that's allowed for an assignment. Rather than asking the teacher for more time, budget enough time for all three steps of writing so you can achieve good quality results with your school writing assignments.

The revision stage is useful to solve all remaining problems in your rough draft. You may find problems with the organization of your material or the development of your theme, and you can return to the planning stage to reorganize supporting material for your weakest points. Sometimes it may be necessary to look for additional information and reorganize the detailed material to improve the quality of your paragraphs. You might rework your writing plan to redevelop some of the subtopics and paragraphs. Return to whatever development stage you need and rework the steps until you reach your goals for the project.

Poor quality papers are only poorly developed and unfinished papers that can be improved enough in this last step to meet reasonably good standards. "Last minute papers" lack the revisions necessary to reach excellent quality with the details of writing. Writing in three steps might seem like more work, but you will find that each step goes quickly and the whole process is faster and easier than struggling to write in one single step. When you have budgeted enough time for all three steps, your written papers will look excellent and earn good grades.

Short and easy papers require only a few readings to check for spelling and grammatical defects that might be missed by computer word processing programs. Long and complex papers require more time for revisions. It takes more time to develop long papers initially, and then it takes more time to revise long papers to meet the higher standards usually required for them. Depending upon your time and goals for the project, continue revising and developing your sentences and paragraphs until you're satisfied with the quality of details in long papers.

Writing styles are growing more casual today to sound like ordinary conversation for most forms of writing, but advanced college papers are graded with formal grammatical standards. Written papers for advanced college courses typically have higher standards for all quality issues. Although you will have more writing experience upon reaching this level, so you can do a better job of organizing and expressing material, it's always wise to check the quality of your details with a grammar guide. Typically, you will need to deal with both the meaning and style of your message for advanced college papers.

It might be sufficient to correct lower level school papers with word processing programs that contain spelling and grammar checking features, but it's wise to check an updated writing style guide about the details for college papers. This insures that your paper meets the requirements for a good grade. Although you can expect to be using the grammar checking features of a word processing program, it's worthwhile checking your details with one or more style guides such as these listed below.

A Few Writing Style Guides

MLA Handbook for Writers of Research Papers, New York: The Modern Language Association of America, 2009.

The Chicago Manual of Style, Chicago: University of Chicago Press, 2003.

Baker, S. *The Longman Practical Stylist,* New York: Pearson Longman, 2006

Writing for Practical Applications
The goal for practical and business writing is organizing your information for efficient reading and applications. Readers must see sufficient organization and summary in practical writing, since this facilitates their understanding for efficient applications. Practical written material is easier to read and apply when the organizing structure has been planned sufficiently.

You might be writing an instruction manual to help others use complex equipment in the workplace, or you might be writing instructions about procedures that you're teaching to others. Otherwise you might be simply writing instructions for taking care of your health concerns at home. For all forms of practical and business writing where efficiency of functioning is important, plan for adequate levels of organization and begin with good quality topic sentences or place titles over the paragraphs.

Plan practical writing with an outline for good organization of the important detailed material. In addition to higher levels of organization, begin your practical writing with a comprehensive introduction and consider ending the paper with a conclusion that presents your recommendations.

Organize subtopics logically and arrange sequences of your detailed material inside paragraphs to facilitate understanding. Check that paragraphs begin with an interesting sentence that summarizes the paragraph topic. When readers fail to notice organizing points and concepts in written material, they will be deficient in understanding and practical functioning. Then readers must use extra time and effort sorting the material and writing adequate study notes to clarify your message, thereby decreasing their time for the applications.

Use more levels of titles to show the organizing structure of your message, since this helps readers to maintain their focus. Try to show key points with titles, and use higher level titles to group these points so it's easy for readers to maintain good orientation for detailed material. Long sentences might begin with the subject to orient readers quickly about the topics. Collections of data might be organized into convenient patterns such as lists, charts, outlines and graphs that help readers to understand and use the data at a glance.

Call attention to your most important points with subtitles, and write one or more paragraphs for each important point. Readers are more likely to notice the important concepts if you present organizing points and concepts with prominent titles. Choose meaningful titles rather than subtle ones. Meaningful titles can be skimmed quickly, whereas subtle titles make readers stop and think, often about distractions. When you show the subtopics with subtitles in practical writing, this helps your readers to maintain their orientation about the topics.

Consider placing a title over each paragraph for the greatest efficiency of reading and applying practical material. Titles over your paragraphs serve as topic sentences so readers don't need to look for summarizing sentences inside of the paragraphs. Titles help readers keep their focus upon the topic, and they help with processing material quickly. Titles save readers the work of sorting material to improve their understanding. Placing a title over each paragraph is a highly effective technique that's useful for many kinds of practical writing.

FORMS OF NOTE WRITING

Many Applications for Note Writing

Reading and Researching – for all forms of reading and studying as described in the previous chapter

Writing and Thinking – collecting your thinking notes and organizing writing plans

Speaking and Listening – for all occasions with important and/or lengthy material

Collecting Daily Journal Notes– for applications requiring systematic note collection

Professional Work – organizing practical knowledge and materials for business and teaching

All intellectual activities work better with note writing, and some of the activities above are impossible without note writing. Your performance with planning writing, speaking and teaching requires organized written notes, and learning from reading and studying can be improved with written notes. All intellectual notes are essentially similar, and they usually consist of a summary or outline of the organizing topics and points to facilitate your thinking about a collection of material. Use summary and outline notes interchangeably for analysis with your many variations of thinking activities.

Studying, writing and thinking are all related activities that depend on organized note writing for very effective functioning. Knowledge generally must be organized around large concepts and subtopics since this facilitates understanding and memory. When you're studying, you need to organize summary notes that show you have identified key concepts and topics. When you're writing, you need to prepare a writing plan that lists the topic and subtopics you want to use for your message and theme. When you're speaking you need to organize detailed material around your concept and subtopics, and begin by summarizing these points to facilitate understanding while listening.

All communication activities require similar mental processes to deal with very large quantities of material efficiently. These processes require the thinking levels of organizing, summarizing and analyzing to create notes for better quality understanding. Students are often unaware of the significant learning power in writing notes for analysis and thinking, so this tool tends to be neglected when studying and writing. Therefore students may find themselves at primitive levels of thinking when they try to write an essay or explain what they learned. Writing organized notes for reading, writing, thinking and speaking contributes the most to your quality of learning and intellectual growth.

Your intellectual growth depends on processing information with written notes for numerous variations of mental activities, especially for learning in higher education. Notes are essential for running a business meeting, for planning a complex business phone call and for saving your ideas from thinking. Students require note writing for better reading and writing, and thinking. Teachers require note writing for teaching, and business workers require note writing for reading, writing and speaking activities. Written notes are tools for all variations of mental activities.

All learning skills are interrelated, and you can improve these skills by writing suitable notes that help you reach higher levels of functioning. Reading notes are important for studying. Writing plan notes are important for preparing organized written papers. Speaking notes are important for an excellent speech that's not disorganized, rambling and also deficient in suitable material. Write listening notes when you want to learn from a long speech that contains important material. Write "thinking notes" by collecting and organizing your own ideas to develop them better. Your speaking and writing skills are related to the quality of your reading and thinking skills. All of these skills are interrelated, and they are all improved significantly by note writing.

Your Thinking Notes
If you sit back and think after reading something, you will get some ideas that are easily forgotten. Writing your ideas clarifies thinking while it facilitates greater development of your ideas and interests. If you don't verbalize or write ideas, they remain vague in your mind and don't function well for your continued thinking. Unwritten ideas are vague fleeting glimpses of material that you might have developed more fully.

"If you can't say it, you don't know it" is a useful expression. Vague ideas floating around in your mind aren't very useful, so you must speak and write your ideas to clarify and develop them. Vague ideas consist of "knowing something" without knowing it very well. On the other hand if you know something fairly well, you should be able to express your understanding with speech and writing. If you neglect the expression of ordinary ideas, it has a negative effect upon your intellectual growth. By using both verbal and written expression, you can improve your thinking and communication skills.

Speech and writing are powerful tools to clarify your thinking and build upon ideas. Although everyday passing thoughts may seem too ordinary to write, you must express and save ideas about your strongest interests so your ideas continue growing. Vague ideas floating around in the back of your mind aren't available for better functioning when they lack development by verbal and written expression. Begin with verbal expression, and then add written expression to save your ideas for continued thinking about topics that you consider important.

Your highest level thinking is facilitated by collecting and organizing reading notes, while also gathering your own ideas with notes. This helps to promote thinking for problem solving, while it facilitates more thinking about your interests. Your note writing for analysis and problem solving is useful for written essays and research papers. Collecting organized notes from research material along with your ideas are the fundamental tools for problem solving with information and thinking, and this process is the key to developing excellent research papers.

Many professional occupations require problem solving and writing about your ideas to clarify and solve problems. The only reasonable way to achieve these goals is by collecting your ideas regularly with thinking notes, also by collecting relevant new information with research notes. Your note collections can be reorganized into writing and speaking plans and into practical applications when necessary. Organizing and saving information collections along with your own ideas is the process that enables you to continue developing critical thinking skills. This provides mental stimulation for more reading and thinking that's essential for developing your learning and thinking skills.

Writing Daily Journal Notes
You might consider writing daily journal style notes as similar to writing a personal diary that's lacking in practical value, but there are important applications for this kind of note collection. For example, doctors and psychologists must collect information regularly about their patients or they won't function very well. Detectives must collect notes about evidence and lawyers must collect material for their cases, or they won't be able to organize information to show connections in the total picture. Reporters must collect sufficient written notes rather than try to remember large amounts of material, and typically they must reorganize the material and write stories about it.

The daily journal style of note collection is useful for many applications. It's essential to collect notes in order to deal with complicated material for business, scientific and legal problems.

Otherwise you're likely to forget many details and fail to see meaningful patterns formed by the consistent collection and organization of information.

If you don't use consistent note collection for the appropriate occasions, your functioning will be deficient. Your collections of notes generally must be written and reorganized into organized arrangements to facilitate analysis of the issues you're trying to clarify. Occasionally it might be necessary to reorganize note collections into many different patterns that meet your various applications. Add suitable headings and labels, with the date and time if necessary, to make your notes easy to use.

Your Speaking Notes

Planning a speech is the same as planning a written paper. Choose your largest concept and subtopics first, then organize enough paragraph topics and detailed material for the speaking time. Speaking notes consist of organized material for specific occasions, and these notes should emphasize the key points of your message. The subtopics are whatever you choose to emphasize and use for organizing suitable detailed material. Your concepts and topics provide summary and organization for detailed material. Use key words to represent the large points, and use phrases to represent supporting points in speech notes, so your speaking sounds spontaneous.

Speaking notes improve your functioning for many occasions, such as sales presentations, interviews, business meetings and phone calls, teaching, discussion groups, and also some informal occasions. Write the same kind of notes to present your own speech that you would write to collect material from someone else's speech. Use the three level outline pattern of topic, subtopics and paragraph topics, organized to show supporting points. Save your speaking notes for related mental activities about the topic, such as thinking and planning writing.

Organizing Speech Material

Your listeners must notice summary and organization for good understanding of your message, since this provides sufficient orientation for processing the material efficiently. Begin speaking with an introduction that summarizes your central concept and subtopics. Follow this summary with detailed material organized around subtopics, and finally conclude with another summary. Your concluding remarks might repeat a summary or present practical recommendations. For important speaking occasions, always present a summary at the beginning and end of your message, emphasizing the central concept and subtopics before presenting detailed supporting material.

When someone is telling you a long and complicated story, it's difficult to pay enough attention to details and remember the material unless the speaker begins with an organized summary. Always begin long spoken messages with summaries, followed by organized information or it's difficult for listeners to process the material. Don't wait until the end of speaking to summarize, especially when your speech contains complicated and lengthy material. Always begin and end with a summary of subtopics, and present detailed material organized around subtopics.

Allow flexibility with speaking notes to adjust the length and content during speaking. Your notes should organize key points with phrases, so they facilitate creative speaking about topics and concepts, allowing flexibility to adapt material to for the time and audience. Then you may add creative thinking or leave out material as time allows. Since you can only estimate the amount of time required for your speech, it's wise to prepare some extra material and keep track of time during speaking. Then if you have more time, add your extra outlined material or else use creative speaking. If your speech is taking more time than estimated, be more concise with detailed material.

Show Your Large Points in Speech
Present speech material so listeners recognize key points versus supporting material. Make your organizing points stand out during speaking so listeners don't fail to notice these points. Outline material with key words and phrases instead of complete sentences, so you can talk about these points with spontaneous sounding speech. Write key words in margins to represent large points. Instead of reading sentences from your notes, just look at the words or phrases and begin speaking spontaneously and creatively. This helps you add current thinking with the outlined material and also provide repetition for key points.

Simply list your subtopics or important points to plan short informal speaking. Now you can say whatever comes to your mind about these listed points during speaking. When a short speech requires formal expression, prepare fully written text for reading, so you can achieve excellent choice of wording along with the appropriate message for the occasion. Then you might use key words to speak your message more spontaneously.

For long and important speaking, fully prepare an outline of supporting material that meets your goals for content and time. Organized speech notes can help with delivering meaningful and spontaneous messages that don't sound like it's being read from written notes. Your outline notes should provide flexibility for explaining your concepts and subtopics with detailed material without losing the organization of supporting points.

Your Listening Notes

Learning from an important speech like a business seminar or college lecture requires note writing to help with your review and memory. Otherwise you won't remember enough later, just like from reading. Outline and summary notes help you learn more from college lectures, from business meetings, and even from popular seminars or videotapes. Writing organized notes helps you keep focused during a speech, and it provides an excellent form of review so you can maintain your memory for thinking about the important points from the message.

Listening notes should look similar to notes you would write for speaking and from reading. The large concepts and subtopics and should stand out from the supporting material, since this promotes good orientation for your efficient review and thinking. Place labels or key words in the margins and underline important points to facilitate efficient review. Otherwise you might write an outline showing the subtopics and supporting points.

Keep your focus during listening by writing summary notes, and you will understand the material better and create excellent review notes. It helps you pay attention and think about the organizing points and relationships, just like excellent reading notes work. Note writing helps you keep track of more material during lengthy or complicated speech. It's unnecessary to write full sentences for your notes, just use phrases and key terms to outline the material, and this helps you organize and keep track of important points in the material.

Improve your comprehension by writing notes to show both summary and organization of the speech. Simply writing the largest points during listening improves your comprehension and memory significantly, but you can learn even more by adding supporting points and important details into an outline pattern as necessary for your goals. Also summarize your notes by adding key words in the margins for easy review.

Review your written notes soon after a speech to check that they make enough sense and will function efficiently for review. Check the organization and readability while you still remember enough to correct your notes. Check to see that you have identified the largest points or subtopics in the speech, and that you have adequately organized supporting points. The specific organization and the amount of detail you want to save will vary with your goals. Written notes should reveal more about the quality of a speech than your note writing ability. When a speech is disorganized or deficient in worthwhile information, your notes should reveal this problem so you may seek more information to fill in deficiencies that you want corrected.

Powerpoint and Handout Notes

The popular trend for speaking and teaching today is bringing your laptop computer with a projector and screen to display a Powerpoint outline of the material. This helps listeners keep their orientation by viewing your organization of subtopics and the supporting points. The alternative is using a blackboard or charts to show organizing points. The Powerpoint computer program helps you organize material in various ways and display it with a projector. If your topic includes complicated material, you can show illustrations, specific data collections and diagrams that help your listeners learn the material.

Another popular trend is preparing "hand-out" notes of your speaking outline so listeners won't need to write so many notes during a complex speech. They can concentrate fully on your message and understand the material better. Occasionally they might take notes about the details not covered in your handout notes. Your Powerpoint display and handout notes promote good orientation for listeners, so they can learn more efficiently when dealing with lengthy or complicated material.

Evaluating Study Courses with Notes

Save study material and written notes to evaluate the knowledge you have gained from college courses. Your course outline or syllabus, along with your reading and lecture notes, books and materials provide a comprehensive view of the knowledge and skills covered. This enables you to evaluate the quality of your knowledge in terms of meeting your functioning needs.

Surveying study materials reveals the extent of knowledge and skills you have gained, so you can decide if your courses have covered adequate material for specific goals and interests. Try to estimate if the knowledge and skills gained is sufficient for your requirements, so that you may correct any deficient areas with additional study on your own. Then you might survey the educational resources available locally, and select information resources that meet your learning goals.

STEPS FOR RESEARCH PAPERS

Three Skills for Research Papers

1) Organize suitable notes with your reading and thinking

2) Apply advanced levels of thinking to form your own views

3) Use good writing strategy to organize your own message

Choosing Forms of Research

Personal research consists of browsing and gathering information for your own interests or practical needs, and this is often the most common research. If you don't bother writing notes, later you might wish you had collected notes or else photocopies because you can't reexamine the information except by going through the search again. It's worth collecting and organizing information for personal interests and writing notes for analysis so you can evaluate the quality of collected material.

Problem solving research is organizing information to answer questions about a topic. Your goal is gathering some relevant information to explore specific interests or solve problems about a topic. You might begin by simply writing a statement to define your inquiry goals. Or else begin by writing planning notes about the topic to organize all of your current information and ideas. This prepares your outline of what you know about the topic, and it helps identify what else you want to learn about the topic. Preliminary planning notes also help you prepare a statement of inquiry and a theme for your written paper.

Lower level research papers are information collections that organize your choice of material about a topic. Most likely you are using computer search engines to gather information that's conveniently available. You might add information from books and magazines to represent a greater variety of resources about the topic. You don't need to collect your own thinking notes, but choose your own subtopics and paragraph points to organize the material and show your personal perspective about a topic.

High school and college level research papers provide some experience with gathering and processing useful information, and they provide opportunities to explore your topics of interest. These papers may combine material from a variety of resources and they should include your thinking notes. All of this material should be integrated into a writing plan that presents your own perspective. If you're using good strategies for developing these research papers, your writing skills will continue growing.

Scientific and medical research uses physical experiments to seek answers to questions. It's essential to define this kind of project clearly in order to design an experiment and collect data that answers questions. Define your research goals by writing a statement of problems or questions to explore, or else by forming a hypothesis. This kind of inquiry should include your problem statement and a reasonable guess or hypothesis about your predicted results. These papers usually present a review of relevant knowledge already written about the topic so you can avoid "reinventing the wheel", and you can build upon what's already known about the topic.

Writing a research paper is similar to writing a small book. Your contribution to knowledge consists of presenting your own unique perspective and viewpoints about the topic. After you have collected material in your interest area, you can reorganize the information while adding your own ideas to improve upon the current level of knowledge and strategy. As a result, the quality of our knowledge is gradually being transformed by this process of reorganizing older material while adding our unique views and perspective.

Writing Research Notes

Your research tools are reading notes, thinking notes and writing plan notes. The most important research skill is writing notes for analysis to apply suitable forms and levels of thinking to your collection of material. Note writing for higher levels of thinking is essential for developing your own viewpoints about the topic. Organize collected notes in patterns that facilitate your thinking and evaluating the key points you found in research material. Then organize a writing plan outline showing your choice of title and subtopics that you're exploring about the topic.

Research reading notes consist of whatever material you may choose to select about the topic. It's unnecessary to analyze all of the material from each resource as required for study notes. Research notes only analyze what you have found of interest or relevance to specific questions that you're exploring. That's why it's so important to begin research projects by organizing your current ideas and material so you can clarify your inquiry goals. Otherwise you might simply survey what material is available about the topic and write a statement of inquiry that provides focus for organizing your perspective about the topic.

Collect your own thinking notes during research reading, so you can add these ideas into your writing plan. Write thinking notes in the margins of your reading notes, or else write large quantities of your ideas on separate pages. Reorganize your collection of notes for analysis and thinking, and to arrange the material in terms of your inquiry goals. Avoid simply stringing together collected material, since this shows lack of your own thinking. You can prevent this problem by combining thinking notes and reading notes and then by reorganizing this material with your own choice of organizing points.

Simple organization of reading notes begins with writing key words in the margins to identify subtopics and paragraph topics. Leave some space for adding your own views along with reading notes that you're collecting. Then you may reorganize all of this material to promote more critical thinking and to develop your own perspective about the material.

Complex organization of research notes requires outlining the material to show your choice of subtopics and related supporting paragraphs. Organize the new connections you're creating about the topic to show your own unique perspective.

Two forms of note organization help manage large collections of material. Write labels in the margins to organize material with your choice of subtopics and paragraph topics. Then save your notes grouped by subtopics so you can easily reorganize the material into arrangements that promote analysis and synthesis. These two forms of organization facilitate restructuring large quantities of reading notes into a writing plan outline.

Easy forms of note collection are being used for reference and online materials. You can print out web pages of information from your computer screen or else use "select, copy and paste" computer functions to copy material and paste it into your own word file. For reference material that can't be taken out of the library, you can take handwritten notes. These forms of note collection facilitate easy sorting with underlining and key words. This provides an opportunity to reexamine material many times and scrutinize details before reorganizing the material into your writing plan. A disadvantage of this note collection is that it's too easy to recopy material without thinking. So make an effort to analyze your collected material with thinking notes.

Write higher level thinking notes to help you develop your own viewpoints about material for written papers. Note writing for analysis and evaluation helps you examine the key concept, the topics and supporting points in collected material, so you can reorganize and combine the material into your personal version. Note writing for synthesis and thinking about new applications of the material helps you develop your own unique problem solving perspective about the topic of interest.

Processing Research Material
Research generally consists of searching for practical knowledge or new perspective about the topic. Stimulating projects might grow out of your current activities or interests that you have been thinking about. You might be searching for interesting or practical information about a topic, or answers to questions or even solutions to specific problems.

Organize your current ideas and information about the topic into a writing plan first. Usually this provides the most effective beginning for written papers. When you outline what you already know about the topic, you can identify what else you would like to learn and what aspects of the topic you want to explore. Therefore begin your writing plan notes before research reading so you can examine current knowledge and views about a topic.

This helps to clarify your interests, while it helps you define the inquiry goals and plan a theme for your writing project.

Write a summary statement to define your research goals, after organizing preliminary planning notes with your current ideas and material. Preliminary notes help clarify the message, making it easier to establish a central concept for your paper. Use your thinking notes and preliminary planning to prepare a summary statement about the topic, so you can use a summary concept to choose your subtopics. This helps with your focus of the message so that you're searching for suitable quality and quantity of material about your central concept.

Two important purposes are served by collecting research material with notes. First, it provides greater coverage of the material about your topic. Second, an equally important purpose served is that it should stimulate more of your own thinking and discussion about the material available about your topic.

A writing plan outline is your most effective procedure for integrating your thinking with collected material. Some points tend to stand out as more important during organizing your collection of material. Find these points that interest you most, and use them to formulate your own points. Choosing your own subtopics and supporting points helps you reorganize collected material in terms of your personal perspective.

Thinking notes for analyzing, evaluating and synthesizing can help you develop your own views with a collection of material. You might begin by analyzing the structure you find in reading material, since this helps you think about the pros and cons. Then you may restructure the topics with additional material to form your own views. This process is essential for synthesizing collected research material into your own unique perspective, so you can choose your own subtopics and paragraph topics to create a unique written message.

Evaluation and synthesis are very important thinking steps for higher level writing. When you understand the concept of using these two key thinking strategies for better quality writing, you can apply these thinking skills more effectively. Begin with analysis so you can perform adequate evaluation and synthesis. You might continue with evaluating and synthesizing material and building upon your writing plan until you reach the level of concept development you want for the message.

Occasionally you must use someone else's written material in your own papers and research projects, so you can build upon what others have written. List the source when presenting or referring to someone else's material. If presenting large amounts of copyright material, get permission from the publisher. For smaller amounts of material, just indicate the source and use quotation marks if you're writing an exact quote. See the *MLA Handbook for Writers of Research Papers* for suitable forms of presenting and documenting the various kinds of reference resources you might use in your written papers.

Your research paper should present a unique theme that provides your own choice of topics about the material, and that emphasizes the most interesting points you have discovered from collecting and analyzing material about the topic. Your goal is presenting relevant and interesting material that you found about your inquiry goals. Always begin research papers with an introduction summarizing your inquiry goals, and end with a practical conclusion presenting the most important points you have discovered and want to emphasize about the topic.

The following procedures are useful for research papers.

Summary of Research Steps

* Organize your current thinking and material about the topic into a preliminary writing plan

* Write a summary statement of inquiry goals or else scientific hypothesis to provide an introduction

* Design a scientific experiment if necessary to solve problems or answer questions

* Collect reading notes for analysis, selecting information in terms of your inquiry goals

* Collect your own thinking notes with reading, and notes from discussion with others

* Write notes for evaluation and synthesis to develop your own thinking about a collection of material

* Estimate the number of paragraphs required for your paper

* List your topic, subtopics and enough paragraph topics

* List supporting points for your subtopics and paragraph topics

* Write an introduction and conclusion that summarizes your key points and conclusions

* Plan separate sections or chapters for very long papers and use subtitles if your subtopics contain many paragraphs

* Check the format required to present reference information used inside your paper

* List the reference resources used at the end of your paper

Consider doing some of these research steps in reverse order when you have limited access to information about your topic. First explore what quantity of material is available for the length of paper you want before defining your inquiry goals and theme. When your location is lacking in access to suitable information, survey the resources and choose your topic in terms of material that you find for the length of your assignment. Collect reading and thinking notes, and build your writing plan until you can organize enough material for your length of paper.

Check all requirements for style and format before organizing your final writing plan, especially for business and scientific style papers. Standardized forms of presentation are commonly used for scientific research. The following headings are often used to organize scientific research. 1) abstract, 2) introduction, 3) methods and materials, 4) results and discussion. Another commonly used format is 1) statement of the problem, 2) background, 3) hypothesis, 4) materials and procedure, 5) data, 6) results, 7) analysis, 8) conclusion. Also business reports may require specific formats. Otherwise see the section about practical writing to present this kind of material effectively.

The biggest research problems are difficulty finding enough material for some inquiries, or else sorting the unusually large quantities of material that are available for some other inquiries. You can increase your research productivity by using summaries and outlines when they are available. An excellent detailed index or table of contents is sometimes as useful as an outline.

Summaries and outlines can help you decide if you want to order specific books for research. Otherwise you must rely upon the small descriptions about books and order them to sort for relevant material. This is very time-consuming for large projects, and therefore most school projects present fairly small samples of material about the topic.

INFORMATION RESOURCES FOR RESEARCH

Searching for Information
In the past research began in libraries and bookstores, but today many information resources are found online with computers. Some resources are no longer found in libraries because they have been entered into computer collections and they are only found by searching the internet with a computer. If interesting or unique information exists about your topic, it's wise to check the internet, in addition to using other materials for research.

Today you can achieve interesting results with research, since you have much greater access to information with the internet. You can sort many library catalogs around the world, numerous magazine articles about any subject, video recordings and many individual web sites that provide interesting material. In the past it would take many years of sorting materials to find enough information for big projects, but today these projects are done more quickly by gathering information from the internet.

One problem with online information is that it's broken down into many subcategories and scattered around into numerous web sites with various arrangements. This creates an impression that a multitude of resources are available. This is confusing for student researchers who might not realize there are only a few large categories of resources online like the library categories. Other web sites are provided by businesses and individuals.

Another problem with online resources is that they are being reorganized and renamed as different web sites more often than you might expect. So use recent internet reference guides when looking for specific web sites. Save reference information about each web site you have used for research. Your reference list for a written paper should include the web site addresses and dates when you have used them to collect information.

Sometimes it's difficult to find outstanding resources online, even though large quantities of information might be available about your topic. Use whatever printed internet guides you can find to help you locate additional resources. If you have the opportunity, check several printed guides about your topic and also check internet research guides that provide information for better quality research. Both the internet and the computer are complex tools, so you can benefit from the use of printed guides to utilize these tools more efficiently for research.

Try to organize a map of your research resources by listing the large categories of information found in your local libraries. Also organize lists of online resources that you have found for research, and save a list of web site addresses that you're most likely to use again for research. These lists can help you locate the kinds of resources you want for specific projects.

Your research can proceed more efficiently if you begin with an orientation to the typical categories of information resources found in your local libraries. When you become acquainted with the largest categories of library resources, you can search more efficiently for these kinds of resources online. Begin by listing the categories of research resources found in local libraries. Below are some common categories of library resources along with their subcategories. Use the list to help you explore these resources in your libraries and online.

Categories of Library Resources

(Some resources are in print and online, others are only online)

Books

Nonfiction; Large libraries have separate departments for their subject matter categories. Use the library classification systems to fully explore subject matter categories and related topics

Fiction; usually organized by authors' names

Biography and autobiography; organized by the subjects' names

Doctor's dissertations and master's level research papers written for advanced college degrees

Reference Books

Dictionaries and Encyclopedias, many are online

General reference collection of books organized by subject areas

Business directories of local and national companies

Collections of phone books, now found online with computers

Specialized collections, such as Consumer Reports publications, auto repair manuals, business investment information, etc.

Maps, picture books and special collections separated by topics

Government Publications

Large libraries keep in separate department, many are online

Periodicals: Magazines and Newspapers

Popular magazines and newspaper articles are listed online or in the Periodicals Index reference book. Older copies of periodicals had been saved as bound books, and now are saved online

Specialized magazines and scholarly Journals. Large libraries and college libraries usually have a greater selection

Local and national newspapers; find more in larger libraries

Video Recordings: CD's and DVD's

Audio tapes and video recordings in the categories of fiction and nonfiction, such as self-help and travel

Movies and Music

Books are the Largest Category

Unless your research is only online, begin by browsing in books at local libraries and bookstores to see if you can find worthwhile information about your topic. You can find greater access to material by going into several large libraries and bookstores. Then you might sort online library catalogs and the web sites of bookstores, but this lacks the access for browsing unless you can find web sites that provide either partial or the full text of books. Otherwise you must order these books from small descriptions and wait to sort them for relevant material.

Most libraries and bookstores have an online web site where you can sort their collections by topics, then order items from home with a library card number. Most libraries combine their book catalogs with their nearby libraries into a regional network catalog, and this provides greater convenience for sorting all of the library collections within each larger region. Also check the libraries in your nearby cities and with local colleges if you want access to browsing among more resources.

Sort library catalogs around the world with your computer at home, or else your local library computer. Simply enter the term "library" and the name of a city and state into a search engine to find the web sites of libraries.

The Library of Congress catalog online provides the most comprehensive list of the book titles published in this country, because they keep copies of all copyrighted materials. However these books are only available for use inside their library, so list what interests you and order the books from other libraries.

World Catalog has the most comprehensive library catalog online, since this combines catalogs from thousands of libraries around the world, including the Library of Congress. When books of interest aren't available from your local library networks, you can order them through World Catalog. These book orders from World Catalog probably take much longer to arrive, so try to order your books from nearby library networks first.

If you want to see older books that are no longer available on library shelves, use the Library of Congress catalog online where you can specify the age range of book titles you want to sort. Otherwise check digital libraries online, since these libraries only provide older titles that you can also read online. Whereas if you only want to sort current books, see "Books in Print" that should be available in your library reference section. Or this might be available online through your library web site.

When sorting books in the library, you have limited access to their collection because some books have been taken out. For a complete list of book titles that a library owns, sort the catalog online and order books you want but can't find on the shelves.

When sorting numerous library catalogs online, copy or print a list of your selections so you can decide later what specific titles to order. First order the books available from your nearby library networks, since these books will arrive much faster. Then you may order books from World Catalog through their web site or else through your local library if they offer this service.

Check for new digital libraries online that provide the full text of books to read. Enter the term "digital library" into any search engine to find web sites that currently provide these libraries. Digital books can be read on your computer screen, or else you can download these books and save them in your computer or print out your own copy. Currently you will find there are very few digital libraries, and these have limited resources, usually only the older books with an expired copyright. Therefore digital libraries are especially useful if you're searching for older books that are no longer available on library shelves.

You can buy low cost used books online when you can't find books that you want locally, or when the books would take too long to arrive from faraway libraries. Many online bookstores sell used books and even new books for low cost, and these book orders usually arrive quickly. You can find a greater selection of books by searching several bookstores online, and this option greatly increases your access to books for important projects. Some web sites even let you resell used books on their site.

Use the library classification systems for help with research. You can find these on the internet and print your own copies. Using these classification systems helps you find related subject matter about your topics. The Dewey Decimal system uses only numbers, while the Library of Congress system begins with letters. Using adequately detailed copies of these systems can help you explore the subtopics and related subject matter fully that you might want to consider when browsing for research.

Reference Books are a Large Subcategory
Reference resources are categorized into general and specialized information. General reference resources contain small amounts of information about numerous topics in books like dictionaries and various encyclopedias and almanacs. Specialized reference resources consist of large collections of information about only one topic, such as financial investments and auto mechanics. These books might be called special collections in the library, or else they are called "databases" online.

Library reference book collections are reserved for use only in the library so they're always available to everyone. For a better selection of these materials, go into larger libraries and also go into more libraries to see if they may have different collections.

Today most reference information can be found online, and you can search by entering your topic in a search engine.

General reference information might be found on many web sites by using the topic or the name of a reference book in any search engine. Try using terms like dictionary, encyclopedia, almanac or phone books. General reference also includes news, weather, travel, maps and many other topics online. Also the web sites of various organizations and businesses may contain small amounts of general reference information.

Specialized reference collections online cover only one topic and they are usually called "databases". You might find some of these collections with the topic or phrase in a search engine. Otherwise try to find an online directory of databases. This topic may be listed in the internet yellow pages, or check information about databases on special reference web sites like "Direct Search", "My Virtual Reference Desk" and the "All-in-One Search Page". Most large databases and web sites provide organized menu lists and a search textbox on their first page.

Web sites about reference material are occasionally changing, but you can check your topic in online directories or in search engines for the web addresses. Popular reference databases are usually available on local library web sites. Many have the group name of EBSCO host, and you can use them at home with a card number. Check with a reference librarian for important projects.

Many large reference databases charge fees to use them, and professional workers purchase these databases for their work, especially the big collections about law, medicine and business. You might consider asking a professional worker to help you find specific information for your research topic, or else you can look for any large reference databases that are free to the public, and it's wise to begin by checking your local library web site.

Government Publications are a Subcategory

Large libraries may have a collection of government publications, but these are usually kept in a separate department from other library materials so it's easy to forget they exist. Otherwise most libraries have some government publications in their reference section, or else you can find these materials listed online on the various government department web sites.

Some libraries don't have government publications available on the shelves for browsing, but you can sort these publications in their online catalog and request to see the items in the library. Try additional libraries if you want to look for these materials on the shelves for browsing. Also sort these collections in several libraries if you want to see a greater variety of titles, or if you want to see more older titles that might be on the shelves.

You will find that government publications are the best source of information about national statistics and also statistics about individual states that you might want for your research projects. Check the web sites of specific government departments if you want to see what publications are currently available for sale. You can purchase these publications online from the appropriate department web sites or from the government bookstore online. Since most government bookstore locations are closed now, you need to order these publications from their online departments, or from the government printing office website at www.gpo.gov. Government consumer information publications can be found at www.pueblo.gsa.gov, organized by the topics.

Periodicals Index of Magazine and Newspaper Articles

In the past this index was a bound set of reference books for libraries called the "Readers' Guide to Periodical Literature", and different sets might be available for specialized topics. These indexes organize the summaries of articles from magazines and newspapers by topics. The older magazines were saved on the library shelves bound into books, and the older newspapers were saved on microfilm so you could read articles that you found in the index. Large libraries usually had a better selection of these reference indexes and they also had a better selection of bound magazines and newspapers saved on microfilm.

Today articles from magazines and newspapers are saved in computer databases. Many libraries provide reference databases on their web sites, and the articles from periodicals may be read online too with your home computer or with a library computer. Otherwise you might subscribe to read specific magazines and newspapers on your home computer. Sometimes this includes the opportunity to research among their past issues.

Periodicals databases might be divided into categories that represent specific topics or magazine collections, so you might need to sort several databases about your topic. The magazine articles are added fairly soon to online collections or else you can see the magazines on library shelves. Most library web sites will provide some reference information databases of periodicals, and you can use them with your library card number.

Separate specialized indexes might be available online for some professional magazines and scholarly topics. Most likely you will find these indexes on college library web sites, and you can use these web sites in the library, or else from home if you have a library card number. The recent magazines can be found on the shelves of college libraries, and large libraries are likely to provide a much greater selection of professional magazines and newspapers that you may use in the library.

Video Recordings, Interviews and Discussion Groups

Often video recordings are neglected for research, but they are valuable resources for some topics. Video recordings, DVD's and CD's, can be sorted and ordered on library web sites or they can be purchased from many bookstore web sites. Library collections contain categories such as movies, music, travel, educational and self-help topics. Video recordings or CD's may be the only resources available for some research topics, but it's necessary to translate verbal and visual material into written notes.

Information and discussion can be found online about many topics of interest in "blogs" or web logs. Your interviews and discussion may provide good research topics, and these are being done online now with email and blogs. Online discussion groups are called "forums" and "chat rooms". Experts may have their own web sites that provide an email address for questions. These resources allow greater access to ideas and material for research. Ideas and information can be shared and discussed around the world as researcher's work on important projects. Computer chat rooms and web logs may stimulate your thinking about important topics, and you can take notes without the need to add your own views on these websites.

You can easily start informal discussions to ask others what they think about topics of interest. Other people might have learned something special about your topic of interest, or they might have different views to add to your collection of material. Perhaps you will have the opportunity to interview a local expert who has developed interesting material or views about a topic. Articles in popular magazines also may stimulate your thinking for essays and research projects. Even reading the "Forum" section of your local newspaper provides views about popular topics that might stimulate your thinking. Write your own ideas and arguments soon after your reading or discussion, so that you're collecting material about your topic.

Conversations with friends, relatives, teachers, neighbors or coworkers might provide ideas for essays and research papers. These conversations may be a source of inspiration for research projects. You might find people with interests or experiences in subject areas related to your topics of interest. Even if you don't find useful material, conversations often stimulate your thinking about many topics. Write your notes from memory soon after conversations have finished, because it distracts others if you write notes during informal conversations. The only requirement is gathering notes from many resources, and also from your own thinking, so this material can be saved and added into personal note collections for your writing projects.

STEPS FOR SEARCHING ONLINE

Methods of Searching Online

Search engines and meta-search engines – enter a topic or several words to see a list of web sites that contain the word or phrase you entered

Web site addresses - enter a web site address to open one web site containing a page or many pages

Web directories and specialized directories - enter a topic and choose from branching to see a list of relevant web sites with small descriptions

Searching online is done with a computer program called an internet program, web browser or search engine. When you open this program, you may see two textboxes at the top of the page. The left textbox is used to enter a web address to open one web site. The right textbox is used to enter one or more words to search for web sites containing these words. Some internet browsers use one textbox to enter both web addresses and search terms. Some textboxes may provide a drop down list of related options when you are typing your terms.

Online information collections are located in many separate web sites, and the methods listed above are used to search for all of these web sites. Some are small personal web sites, many are business and educational institution web sites and others are large collections of reference information called databases. You can find all of the library information categories online, such as books, reference information, government publications, articles from periodicals and video recordings.

Web site addresses can be found in several ways. You can use printed web guides, or use the list of web sites you find with a topic in search engines. Also business directories and phone book yellow pages, online and printed, may include web site addresses for the businesses listed. Web site addresses are organized by topics in the internet yellow pages. The largest category of web sites is commercial, and these sites represent businesses, schools, organizations and all related categories that you can find in phone books and business directories. Also you can find many web site addresses by entering descriptions or the product of a business into search engines.

Web directories contain lists of web sites sorted by experts for relevance to the topics listed. Open any web directory and click on your choice of topic to find branching into subtopics, and more branching into lists of individual web sites with small descriptions. Although search engines bring up many more web sites about your topic, the web sites listed in an online directory focus on higher quality material about the topic. Web directories may be found on reference web sites about specialized topics, and you may find specialized directories on "refdesk.com".

Some search engines have web directories. The best known web directories are located at "yahoo.com" and "google.com". The Yahoo homepage contains a link to their directory. On the Google homepage, click on "more..." to find a link to their directory. Sometimes web directories are called information clearinghouses, since they organize links to related web sites about their topics. Specialized subject directories are available for some topics, and they might be found by using your search topic along with the term "web directory".

Sometimes web directories called "clearinghouses", since they provide links to good quality web sites about your topic. Specialized directories are stepping-stones for increasing your productivity, since they organize some relevant information and identify useful web sites for your topic. Also, try using whatever printed web guides you can find in order to explore an even greater selection of web sites about your topic.

Search engines are also called indexes of the web and their unique quality is that you don't need to know web addresses to find web sites about your topic. Simply enter a term or phrase about the topic or kind of business, and search engines bring up a list of the web sites containing your search terms. Each web site listed shows a web address and small description of the web site. Sort these descriptions, and open web sites most likely to contain the kind of information you want. You can print web pages of interest for your research notes, or else you can "copy and paste" sections into computer word files.

Several different search engines might be loaded into the search textbox of your internet browser. Click on the left icon of this textbox to see a drop down list and choose a search engine. If you don't have multiple search engines loaded into this textbox, you can enter the web address of any search engine into your web address textbox. For additional information about using search engines effectively for better quality research, try using some printed guides for internet research.

Some search engines provide a "portal page" as their first page. This page contains convenient links to other web sites with resources that may be of interest to people searching the web.

Some popular portal pages might be found at "yahoo.com" and "msn.com". Sometimes you can revise portal pages to display links to other web sites that you're most likely to be using again. Some web sites escape being listed with online directories and search engines, and web sites like "invisible web.com" claim to be able to find some of these hidden sites.

Generally search engines list more web sites than you want to sort, even with carefully refined or advanced search terms, and many of these web sites may be lacking good material for your interests. After sorting about forty or fifty web sites, your chance of finding suitable material for your topic is diminishing, depending upon how thoroughly you want to sort.

Explore more material online by using more search methods. Trying more search engines and more search terms and phrases helps you find more web sites. You may see a different variety of web sites coming up at the top of listed web sites when you try more search engines and search terms. Also it's worthwhile to try meta-search engines that combine the capacities of many search engines into one, such as "metacrawler.com".

Trying more search terms brings up many more web sites to sort, but you need to evaluate the quality of individual web sites because some web sites contain poor quality information or may even be deceptive. Generally you can trust the information on web sites of large well-known organizations, but the information on small individual web sites might be unreliable. Sometimes web information may be intentionally false and misleading, so you need to be wary about this problem.

Collect reference information about all of the web sites you're using for a written paper. For web references, include each web address with a small description. Also list the date when you have used each web site for your research, since web sites might be changed anytime. Avoid presenting web site material as your own material in written papers. Always indicate the source or the website in parenthesis, adding quotation marks for exact quotes. Check the style guides for writers of research papers to see what format is recommended for presenting reference and web site material inside your written paper and for presenting resources you have used in your reference list.

Using the common search tools online may seem inefficient, so it's worth trying to find up-to-date web guides and special web sites that organize information about your topic. Also it's worth checking internet research guides for help with using the internet for higher quality research. Sometimes it's difficult to find the best web sites about your topic, because you might need updated information or unique terms to find web sites that have reorganized and changed their addresses.

Summary Steps for Writing

Estimate the number of pages and paragraphs you want

Organize your current ideas before gathering reading notes

Collect your own thinking notes along with reading notes

Label your notes with paragraph topics to organize material

List your topic, key points or subtopics and paragraph topics

List enough paragraph topics to create the length of paper

Outline collected material and thinking notes for paragraphs

Summarize each subtopic with a paragraph or subtitle

Write discussion for your paragraphs with outlined material

Organize an introduction of your inquiry goals for the paper

Long papers might have an introduction and conclusion

Reread and revise to improve the quality of your details

Consider using subtitles for papers longer than five pages

3 GOALS AND TIME

Goals and Time Steps

PLANNING goals and activities organized by topics

ORGANIZING information, paperwork and materials

SCHEDULING to organize time for priority activities

EVALUATING progress and new information to update your planning

ORGANIZING GOALS

Higher level achievement requires planning and time scheduling. Symptoms of inadequate planning consist of vague thinking about your options and failing to use time well. You might have vague ideas for goals, too much wasted time, poorly organized materials and a random approach to activities. Planning provides your ideas and organization for greater achievement and all age groups can benefit. You can gain greater efficiency and a sense of direction in life by identifying your interests and goals and by listing your planning ideas and scheduling time.

Planning and scheduling are tools for greater achievement as a student in higher education and whenever you want better quality functioning. The greater your study workload or goals, the greater your need for planning and scheduling. Although it takes time to plan your activities, it saves much more time since less time is wasted consistently. Substantial benefits are possible by occasionally writing planning lists. For greater benefit, list all categories of your concerns and choose priorities so you can plan for the best use of your time and energy.

Four steps listed above are basic procedures for organizing productivity in business, and they are equally effective for high achievement in education. Workplace productivity depends on organizing and coordinating planning, information and materials in all categories that are essential for the business functioning.

Business planning may include research for useful information, and these topics might be divided into separate departments for management. However the four steps listed above contain the basic organizing procedures that are essential for managing all forms of productivity, both business and personal.

Organization is an underlying strategy for the management of productivity, using the four steps listed above. These steps are the primary methods of organization in business, and they are equally effective steps for managing all forms of achievement. Separately each step is an ordinary tool, but used in combination they provide a comprehensive system for managing complex activity. The four steps for organizing productivity can help you manage personal goals as effectively as a business and they are the most valuable steps for increasing your achievement.

The following concepts presented in this chapter can help you get organized for greater achievement.

* **Four steps used for organizing business productivity work equally well for personal achievement**

* **Identify all categories of concerns and plan for your priority activities**

* **Written planning and records are tools for managing complex patterns of activities**

* **Organization is the underlying strategy for efficiently managing all forms of complex activities**

Planning or Random Wandering
Travelers often plan and schedule a daily or weekly agenda to cover preferred activities instead of wandering around randomly. Life is like random wandering without planning and scheduling that helps you avoid the boredom of too many unplanned days. Randomly you will tend to get some good ideas about what you want to do, forget about them, and then occasionally remember them later. This doesn't work well for important goals, because you need a method for keeping track of activities consistently. When you're only doing random activity, then you aren't doing enough things that are very important to you or even things that you would enjoy the most.

Instead of random wandering try to identify preferred options in each stage of life and write lists and schedules to reach all your preferences and goals. Many goals depend on managing long and short-term planning and scheduling. Without planning for long-term goals, you won't have the opportunity for reaching possibilities that are only attainable by your consistent planning. Without planning for the short term, your weekly and daily activities will tend to be random and disorganized. Improve your quality of life with long and short-term planning that can help you identify and organize your preferences and goals.

When you get a good idea for an activity, usually it's not a convenient time for the activity. Likewise, you might fail to get good ideas for activities when you're bored and have time for preferred activities. Therefore, collecting ideas for activities and goals and planning time usage improves the quality of your life. For various categories, write lists of your preferences and goals. Identify what you want to achieve, what activities you want to emphasize for recreation and the routines you want to establish for efficiency, so you don't have to stop and think frequently about what to do next.

Consider the multitude of possibilities you might explore by collecting planning ideas and by comprehensively thinking about these options. Although you might neglect planned activities sometimes, at least it's your decision from organized planning rather than simply random. If you choose to neglect planned activities, at least you will be much wiser from exploring your possibilities. Unless you stop and think about planning options occasionally, and list your current ideas, you may fail to discover your most preferred options and you may fail to make enough good things happen for yourself.

Lack of Planning

Planning is equally important for managing higher education and for managing business goals. Managing your educational goals with planning and scheduling is totally your own responsibility. You will be considered a poor manager of your life if you don't pay attention to identifying your goals and tracking progress. Simply knowing about procedures for planning and scheduling might satisfy your curiosity, but you need to apply effective procedures to reach greater educational achievement by getting organized with planning and time scheduling.

You may be too dysfunctional for high levels of achievement if you lack the organizational strategies for managing education. You may fall behind with reading assignments, neglect written papers until the last minute, and your testing days may depend on all night cramming. Students with large workloads in higher education can benefit greatly from writing planning lists for their activities and scheduling enough time for study. Planning and scheduling provides the assurance that your work gets done, and that your achievement goals are being accomplished within the recommended time schedule.

"Those who fail to plan, plan to fail" is a popular expression among business managers. In the workplace managers must take responsibility for keeping track of business goals, but you will be considered an inferior employee if you don't contribute adequately towards achieving those goals. Planning is essential for greater achievement in business, and then it becomes an evaluation tool for measuring how well the business is doing and how well employees are contributing to the goals.

Thinking about your options helps you identify better ways of using time in addition to dealing with your achievement goals. You won't even enjoy leisure time as much as possible unless you plan for some preferred activities. Instead of complaining that life is boring and there's nothing to do, improve the quality of your life by identifying preferred goals and activities. You can create a more productive and enjoyable life, even when your planning is only tentative or optional.

Choose Planning Categories
Take a comprehensive approach to planning, so you don't wait to accidentally discover your important goals. First choose your largest categories of planning concerns and list some general ideas to get started. Then improve your planning over time by collecting information and thinking about options and interests. Excellent planning depends on collecting information and ideas, evaluating options and choosing priorities. You might consider writing separate planning lists for your definite goals versus for collecting ideas that you want to consider and evaluate.

Planning helps you clarify primary goals, secondary interests and identify priorities. Otherwise you may randomly spend too much time and money on things that are not important to you. Planning helps you determine how to best manage the limited resources of time and energy for your highest level concerns. Writing lists of planning ideas and identifying priority activities keeps you focused on your achievement goals.

When you ask people about their New Year's resolutions, the replies are usually vague. When you ask this question about specific categories of activities, then most people seem to know immediately what they want to accomplish. You can become more thorough and systematic with your planning by listing all of the categories and topics you want to consider. Otherwise you may be left with a nagging sense that something is missing, and your most important concerns might very well be missing from the topics you're using for planning.

Choosing your planning categories is the first step for getting organized. If you have simple planning lists with very few items, then you have very little need for scheduling time and organizing materials for efficiency. If you have long lists and complex goals, it's wise to get organized in many ways that can increase your efficiency of functioning. Also review your planning categories and activities occasionally so you don't discover too late that you could have been using your time in better ways.

Many people focus too much on some activities in their lives, and they lack adequate focus on other very important concerns. You can prevent this problem by listing the categories you want to consider for planning. Organize comprehensive planning by choosing your largest categories and topics first. This helps you take a balanced view of planning and identify your priorities. Begin with your highest level of concerns, dividing the largest categories into subtopics for planning in greater detail.

Four common planning categories are listed below, and you can build upon them to cover all of your concerns.

EDUCATION PLANNING STEPS

Education – plan for career goals, for alternative work options and for personal interests

Knowledge and Skills – consider educational goals for career preparation versus for personal interests

Extra Reading and Research – consider what books you want to read and what topics you want to research

Homework for School or Career – schedule time for activities that increase your educational achievement

WORK PLANNING STEPS

Career – prepare for a category of work with related options

Future Promotions - consider your goals for future promotions

Alternative Work - consider and list your various work options

Entrepreneurship – collect business ideas you want to evaluate and consider

BUDGET PLANNING STEPS

Financial – write annual and monthly budget summaries for your long-term and short-term planning

Monthly and Weekly Budgets – keep records of spending in terms of your categories of expenses

Savings and Investments – savings for emergency fund, for retirement and other goals

Large Purchases - house and car, and planning for repairs and replacement of large items

Household Budget – distribute your expenses into categories such as food, shelter, utilities, transportation, clothing, etc.

Household Maintenance – house and car maintenance

SELF MAINTENANCE PLANNING STEPS

Self-care Routines - menu planning and grocery shopping, washing clothes and household cleaning

Health Concerns - schedule medical check-ups and an exercise program, collect updated health information

Emergency Plans- smoke alarms for household security, auto breakdown on the road and weather emergencies, etc.

Family Relationships and Friendships – planning for holidays and special occasions and visiting

Recreation and Travel - planning travel for weekends or else week-long vacations, hobbies, sports and entertainment

Written Records for Planning
Writing lists for planning works like magic to keep your focus, or else it's too easy to forget planning ideas. Written planning helps you explore your interests and concerns more fully, so you don't focus exclusively upon favorite activities while neglecting other concerns for the bigger picture in your life. Occasionally thinking about your options and collecting ideas is essential for clarifying goals, finding better ways of using time, and moving forward with developing your interests and goals.

Regularly writing planning is better than frequently wondering what to do next. Even simple ideas for daily activities tend to be forgotten without a simple list. Without written planning you will tend to be disorganized and waste time. Lists are your tools and records for thinking and planning, evaluating and scheduling, and they help keep your focus on planned activities. Written lists help you keep track of your ideas and activities so you will tend to function much more productively.

Long-term planning begins with collecting information and ideas for long-term goals. Instead of simply making New Year's resolutions, annually review your long-term planning more fully. Long-term plans require more time for thinking and evaluating these options to make better decisions. Occasionally reconsider your planning options, so you're taking more time to evaluate the options for important categories. Long-term goals require a greater investment of your time, so an annual review helps with reconsidering these important goals and activities.

Short-term planning covers activities for shorter time units, such as monthly, weekly and daily. Your lifestyle might be too boring and disorganized in the short-term if you don't write some planning ideas for short-term activities. Begin by listing your choice of categories for planning these short time units, including self-maintenance activities, favorite hobbies and your choice of recreation. Many topics from long-term planning may contain items for short-term scheduling, so these items can be simply carried over from long-term lists. Review these options on a monthly basis to schedule activities for the month.

Establish self-maintenance routines so that regular activities are performed automatically, and so they require less attention. This saves time and energy with the activities you want repeated regularly. If you must stop and think about what to do next, and overcome inertia and procrastination for boring routine activities, then it takes more effort. You might post a schedule to help remember your routines, especially for busy patterns and to help younger family members remember their routine schedule. Routines make life easier, as long as they don't take too much time and energy away from your priority activities.

Collect planning ideas while you're thinking about them, or else good ideas are easily forgotten. Later these ideas can be organized by categories and topics and placed on planning lists. You might change your mind and cross off some items from your lists, or you might transfer some items to different categories. For example, if you happen to think about a specific item of work that should be done, write it under the appropriate category in your notebook. Then you won't forget to include this item when you're scheduling monthly or weekly activities.

Small notebooks are handy to carry around or keep on your desk for collecting ideas. Otherwise write ideas as they occur to you on convenient paper and add them to planning lists later. You might organize planning lists by topics in a small notebook, using stick-on divider tabs for different sections. One section might contain ideas that you're saving to think about, while another section might contain lists of your monthly and weekly work goals. Another section may contain a suggested schedule that you carry around to keep track of your many daily activities. Lists work better than trying to remember numerous items, and they serve as your reminder for time scheduling.

Collect Information for Planning

Search for current and useful information for planning categories that can be improved by collecting and evaluating information. Information collections are essential for improving planning in your most important categories. Also when your planning grows more complex, it's worthwhile gathering and organizing relevant information. Organize the material into suitable note patterns for your thinking goals and practical applications.

Simple lists work well to organize planning for most concerns, but when activities become complex, coordinate your planning with suitable information collections. For example when planning a special occasion, list all categories of items for your planning. List current ideas for each category of options before collecting information to improve planning. Gather suitable information for each category of items in order to evaluate and choose from your options. You might keep track of progress with a check list of items that you have completed.

Procedures for business planning are useful to improve upon personal planning. Complicated business problems often require collecting and evaluating relevant and up-to-date information for planning. This kind of planning requires regular updating to keep up with changes in the marketplace and new knowledge about business products or services. These procedures are also useful for some forms of personal planning, such as planning financial investments, applying health information, developing your own business plans, or taking a more complex approach to dealing with some ordinary everyday concerns.

Steps from the research process can be used to improve your planning strategies and achieve much better quality functioning. Problem definition is the first step from the research process. Begin by clarifying your problems with written descriptions. Gather your current thinking and information about problems in an organized and comprehensive form before searching for useful information. Collect information for problem definitions, and use suitable forms of note writing to help apply adequate levels of analysis. These procedures are important to deal with complex problems, and they also help you improve the planning for some of your ordinary concerns.

You might continue with collecting and evaluating information long term, since you can develop better solutions by taking more time with complex decisions. Problems that require long term analysis and development of strategies depend upon organizing suitable information, and you might continue adding information to update your planning. Most likely you will continue thinking about and evaluating important topics when planning your long term interests and goals.

Steps for Using Information in Planning

1) Problem definition, suitably organized and written

2) Organize notes with current ideas and information

3) Gather and evaluate new information for the problem

4) Organize information in practical patterns for application

Choosing Your Priorities

People tend to focus on some interests while neglecting other concerns in their lives. When evaluating your options, decide how much emphasis to place on each planning topic and what achievement goals are most important to you. Maximize the value of your time by identifying your priority concerns that require more focus. Instead of learning your lessons the hard way in life, learn your lessons the easy way with comprehensive planning that helps you identify and maintain adequate focus on your most important concerns and interests.

Some activities are always considered higher priority when planning and scheduling. It's useful to identify these items in your planning. You can underline or check mark priority items and place your optional items in parentheses. When your most important items are marked in some form, it helps you maintain focus on these items. If extra time is needed for priority items, you can use some time from optional items. You might find it helpful to check mark the finished items on your schedule to help you can keep track of progress for important goals.

A common planning problem for young people is the lack of wisdom they tend to get later in life. Most likely they will look back on some of their youthful decisions as being poor quality. People begin developing wisdom by age forty and might not reach their highest levels until age sixty or later. However it's not wise to wait until older ages to begin planning. Instead it's wise to discuss planning ideas with others, especially with older people who may have learned valuable lessons from experience. Also discuss planning ideas with others who might help you consider the pros and cons of your options.

It's worth learning about planning when you're young, even though you might need help from others. It's worth collecting ideas and evaluating planning options even when your goals are only tentative. You can learn more at any age from discussion of planning topics and categories with others who have different views and experiences, since discussion stimulates your thinking for evaluating the options and finding your priority goals.

Planning Study Goals

When you only schedule time sessions for study, you might not notice that you're working slowly and taking random rest breaks. It's better to set goals about how much work you expect to finish during each session and each day before taking rest breaks. Otherwise you might "take it easy" during study sessions and not finish your work. Setting goals for each study session and for each day pushes you to keep busy and finish your work.

Set small work goals that you must finish before small rest breaks, and use these goals to keep busy and even hurry toward your rest breaks. Instead of taking random rest breaks that waste too much time, take small breaks to summarize the material. Use these small breaks during reading to look up and summarize each paragraph and section. This pattern encourages you to keep busy instead of taking only random rest breaks. Don't take a small break until each small unit of work is done. This forces you to keep busy and finish your work on schedule.

Tell yourself that you must read one paragraph or unit of material before taking a small break. Then take a tiny break by summarizing the material and looking away for a moment. Take larger rest breaks after each larger section by writing a summary or underlining the largest topics and supporting points. Read the whole chapter this way and organize complete summary notes before taking a larger rest break by walking around and getting a drink. This procedure encourages you to keep busy and avoid random rest breaks, so you can finish your scheduled assignments within a reasonable amount of time.

Your work gets done efficiently and on schedule when you're keeping busy with a pattern of small goals and small rest breaks. Otherwise you might procrastinate about working during your study sessions, and waste too much time with random breaks. Try to read one paragraph before taking a small rest break to summarize the topic. Try to finish numerous small work goals before taking a larger rest break. Generally you can expect to read one chapter during a session unless it's a difficult chapter. Then take a walk or longer rest break before beginning another session to resume your scheduled activities.

List your total study workload for each week and each day, and distribute this workload in your time schedule for the week. Also schedule some time for your other activities, such as daily recreation and exercise. It works better to use a checklist along with your schedule to keep track of finishing your priority work. When you have long lists of work to finish, you can keep track of progress by checking the work off your list when it's done.

Planning Budget Goals

Student budget planning consists of identifying your options and choosing goals. Include budget planning along with your regular annual and monthly planning or else this category may fail to get enough attention. A practical goal is keeping track of your spending so that it doesn't get out of control, and this prevents problems from developing with debt. The higher level goal is planning the best use of your financial resources and finding ways to avoid overspending and maximize savings, since this increases your ability to deal with unexpected expenses.

Write an annual and monthly budget sheet that you can use for planning your budget goals, and for tracking your expenses and spending activities with written, organized records. Written records of financial activities provide the information you need for budget planning. When you keep track of expenses with written records, you can focus on your priorities and avoid overspending in some categories. Sometimes financial decisions are influenced by temporary moods, but this is much less likely to happen when you keep track of spending with written records and review your financial planning goals occasionally.

A financial balance sheet is the primary planning tool for individuals and businesses. This sheet summarizes your annual activity for all categories of expenses and income, so it shows "the big picture" to help you decide the best distribution of your financial resources. Organize all of your activities by categories under the two headings of "expenses" and "income", and the total amounts under each of these headings should balance or be the same. It's always wise to include a category for savings under the heading of "expenses". Then if you want to show more detailed planning, add subtopics to your categories.

Categories on your balance sheet help you decide how much you can afford in each category, and how much you can place in savings each month. Use separate categories for your "fixed expenses" versus "optional spending" so you can plan for the best use of extra money. Include a miscellaneous category on your balance sheet, since there are always unexpected expenses that don't fit the other categories. Over time your miscellaneous list of expenses will show how much money you generally need to set aside for this category. It's wise to keep enough money in an emergency savings fund to cover the miscellaneous expenses that tend to occur occasionally.

Write a monthly budget summary showing how your money is being used on a monthly basis. This provides the information you need to keep within a reasonable budget and to focus on priorities. Begin with record keeping about your expenses and purchases, and organize all categories of monthly spending on your budget sheet. If your financial information is incomplete, keep track of spending activities for a few months or a year and a complete picture will emerge. A monthly budget sheet helps you plan how to best distribute your money among categories, and thereby plan the best use of your money.

Even if you lack good ideas for budget planning right now, good strategies can be developed over time by collecting ideas and information. Consider how each budget category might be improved upon by weighing your options and evaluating your alternatives. After some time of record keeping you will discover how much to budget for each category of expenses, and you will discover any overspending in categories that can be improved by keeping track of spending activities and by reevaluating your budget planning occasionally.

The best method for controlling your budget consists of keeping records of spending and expenses and writing planning before spending for some categories. When your complex planning is written, you can take more time to weigh these options and find opportunities for saving in ways that you wouldn't notice without taking the time for writing lists and thinking.

Budget planning consists of clarifying your long-term goals and managing short-term activity. Begin by identifying your expenses, organizing written records of categories of spending. Review your planning and progress annually and monthly, so that over the long term the quality of your budget planning will improve so you gain greater value from these resources.

Household and Group Planning
Group planning consists of individuals dealing with their common concerns by planning together for goals and activities. This kind of planning is useful for families, classrooms, business meetings, friendship groups, and in many other situations where groups might gather. Individuals who participate in this kind of planning and decision making with others tend to be more productive and cooperative members of the group.

Begin planning efficiently by listing the categories of concerns from each group member. Gather ideas from members about what they prefer for goals and activities. The leader may collect ideas in a notebook at meetings. Also individual members may collect ideas and information about their concerns so they can share collected ideas and material with others at the meetings. Information collections might be organized by categories and topics that facilitate group discussion. Save written records since they are essential to keep track of goals and activities for the group, and later they are useful to build upon planning.

Young people need help with planning better activities. You can see them looking bored during summer vacation. If you ask them what they like to do, and get them thinking about activities, you will find they have plenty of interests and ideas about what they would like to learn and achieve. However if no one is helping them with planning and scheduling, they tend to simply waste time and suffer from too much boredom. Young people who lack planned activities spend too much time with TV and video games. Many would prefer a greater variety of activities, but it just doesn't occur to them how to plan and schedule for better quality activities.

Children can have better quality activities and choose goals if they have help with planning and scheduling. Otherwise they tend to have disorganized lives and lack opportunities for good quality activities. Begin with scheduling some routine items, and then collect ideas and list categories of their planning concerns. Choose their best ideas for priorities, since they might not have time for all of the options on their list.

When teenagers participate in planning, they choose more interesting activities and better quality learning experiences. Sometimes teens get into trouble because they are keeping company with others who have poor quality ideas for activities, leading the group members to participate. Discuss this problem and help teenagers plan and schedule better activities to prevent this risk. Write schedules to help teenagers or family members remember their planned activities, so instead of depending on reminders from others they can learn to check their schedule.

It's beneficial for young people to discuss planning topics with people around them who can help them gain wider perspective. Most planning topics are good conversational topics, and people enjoy discussion about these topics. Young people can collect ideas and organize notes for planning about topics of interest.

Young people and teens achieve more when they have to earn their spending allowance and some rewards for extra work. Instead of providing everything free while they are being lazy or poorly behaved, assign some important goals to earn rewards. They can earn allowances by cooking and cleaning and other household work. They might be rewarded for good grades, doing better homework and some extra reading. Young people might enjoy helping to plan healthy menus, and also plan vacations and entertainment as rewards for achievement.

Include young people in family group planning so they learn about planning from experience. They can start a notebook for their own planning ideas. Group planning can help household members share the work of running their household, managing their budget, and also planning for some recreation. Each group member can help with choosing activities for all of the members to participate. This kind of planning promotes better attitudes while it helps members learn planning and scheduling so they can deal with their own planning concerns effectively.

Family planning provides an opportunity to discuss important topics such as education, careers, financial planning, health and entertainment. Ask family members about their concerns they want to discuss and manage with planning. Otherwise planning might cover fairly random concerns and fail to focus sufficiently upon each person's highest priority interests. Collect notes about your planning ideas and relevant information collections, or else this material tends to be forgotten.

Steps for Problem Solving in Groups

* Each member contributes problem-solving ideas to a list

* Group discussion about listed ideas and choose solutions

* Research for information to improve planning if necessary

* List activities to implement planning and schedule time

Spare Time Reading Goals

The largest part of your knowledge is gained outside of school, and your knowledge is continually growing. You can consciously direct the course of your learning by setting personal goals for reading and research. Consider what knowledge and skills you would like to develop, and what interests and hobbies you want to explore. These interests might be different from your career goals, but they will tend to show your strongest preferences. Although it might take time to discover all of your interests, you can get started by choosing some spare time reading.

During life you will continue learning for personal interests and goals. This learning might reveal your strongest interests, and it might hold your greatest rewards in terms of developing unique skills. Instead of leaving this category to random chance, consider setting goals for extra learning and set out spare time reading material. Eventually your extra learning may lead to significant practical applications. When your strongest interests aren't being used for your career activities, most likely they will become your favorite hobbies.

Spare-time learning tends to be overlooked during planning, but this category tends to contain your strongest interests and rewards. It's worth setting goals for spare time reading. Locate and organize materials you want to read when you have time.

You can explore personal interests and develop expertise in your choice of subject matter, or else just browse to increase your general knowledge. Collect and save information for your strong personal interests with organized notes so that you're continuing to build knowledge about topics of greatest interest.

Considering Rest and Recreation

Wise people said it's possible to over plan your life and goals. Some plans need to simply unfold according to your developing interests and talents. Some options are waiting to be discovered by you later. Also you might have heard people say, "I don't have time to think." It's a good definition of being excessively busy, indicating a need to cut back on your planned activities so you have enough time for relaxation and thinking. Although it's clearly wise to set goals and strive for reasonable levels of achievement, it's equally wise to balance your planned activities with adequate rest and recreation.

Consider leaving time to have rest, recreation and reflection. It's worth thinking about what's a reasonable load of activities for you at this time, and then leave some free time and flexibility in your schedule to allow for spontaneous activity and thinking. It's an issue to weigh so you don't become over scheduled, but leave enough flexibility in your schedule to include reasonable amounts of time for rest, recreation and reflection.

You might have strongly preferred goals that require more time for achievement activities. Or else you might go through a busy phase during your life when reaching higher achievement goals is more important to you than having more free time. However you would not choose this condition on a regular basis, unless you have strong goals and prefer working on them rather than having free time. This can be your choice from planning rather than from unintentionally over-scheduling. Consider that some achievement goals might result in a very busy lifestyle, and that it's difficult to change course once your path has been established with a series of long-term decisions.

Creativity, Change and Risk

Seek balance between being productive through organization, versus being creative through spontaneous activity. Both of these elements are important for personal growth and progress, and there's always an element of unpredictability in life that might change your circumstances, regardless of planning.

Stop to think about unexpected events that might affect your planning, since there are limitations to what you can control entirely by yourself. Although you might need to deal with unexpected twists of fate, you still need to make good things happen for yourself in terms of what you know about and what you can control in your life. Although the future is unpredictable in some ways, you can't sit around waiting for random events. Instead, you can definitely plan for the typical and expected events in life and even plan for some of the known risks.

Risk management is commonly used for the large categories of health, finance and expensive possessions. These categories can be estimated and managed with suitable insurance. The easiest category is material possessions since we usually have insurance for expensive items like houses and cars. The health category is managed with insurance and avoiding injuries from accidents. Manage financial security by maintaining an income, planning for reasonable savings and then by financial planning and budgeting for your other personal concerns.

Gain more security by keeping an emergency savings account for unexpected expenses during your school and working years. Usually students must live within a very limited budget, but they tend to spend most of their money without any budget planning. So they may run out of money when dealing with unexpected expenses. Financial planners generally recommend keeping an emergency savings fund for at least several months of expenses. Your emergency fund should cover temporary loss of income, unexpected bills, automobile repair and miscellaneous expenses. You might even want to consider setting aside additional savings for weather disasters that could result in your unexpected and unplanned evacuation for a week or more.

ORGANIZING MATERIALS

Easily Organizing Material Things
Instead of wondering what you have in each category and how you might function better, organize and coordinate materials with your activity patterns. Wasting time and energy dealing with disorganization is as inefficient as trying to remember what you should be doing next instead of writing some planning lists. Only small amounts of time are required to organize personal collections, compared to the large amount of time consistently wasted in searching for items. Even simple efforts to organize personal things can save substantial time and energy, while significantly improving your quality of functioning.

You might not notice being disorganized in some ways, since many things are organized for us by common lifestyle standards. Consider that furniture sets are designed for each kind of room. Your cooking supplies are generally kept in the kitchen, and your tools are kept in the garage or basement. Unfortunately it's your remaining collections, and especially paperwork, that's usually disorganized. A common concept of getting organized is simply cleaning out clutter, but this won't produce good enough results for your best quality of functioning.

Personal items are easily organized for your convenience, compared to the large volume of items found within businesses. The value of good organization becomes clear if you compare businesses and homes. Good organization is required in many categories for businesses to function well, since large quantities of items and information are too complex to manage unless they are highly organized. You can increase your efficiency with many activities by organizing personal materials. Also this helps with using your living space more effectively in terms of planning the furniture arrangements and storage containers.

Create organization by grouping your similar items together. For small quantities of items, keep similar items or papers in one container. For large quantities of items, divide your items into subcategories and store them in separate containers. Label the containers when storing large quantities of materials, also arrange materials for convenience with your activity patterns. For complex patterns of activities, write inventories of your materials and activity patterns to keep track of everything for better quality organization and functioning.

Steps for Organizing Material Things

1) Categorize and group similar items together to show all of your options within each category and group. Discard any unwanted and unused items during sorting.

2) Select storage cabinets and containers to arrange items in your living spaces. If you have too many items for your storage containers, then use long-term storage areas.

3) Miscellaneous containers or drawers are always required for small quantities of items that don't belong with any of your groups and categories.

4) Arrange materials for efficiency with your activity patterns, placing frequently used items in front, less frequently used items behind, and rarely used items in long-term storage areas that are out of the way.

5) Occasionally reorganize materials to include new acquisitions and discard unused items. Write inventories to keep track of large quantities of materials efficiently.

Household organization is arranging items for convenience with your activity patterns and living space and storage units. After categorizing and grouping your materials, you can see what quantity of storage furniture and containers you need to arrange the materials for your activities. Keep your organization reasonably simple. When organization is unnecessarily complex, it takes too much time and energy to manage. Arrange your materials by simple categories and groups. It meets your need for efficient functioning, and it won't require an excessive amount of time and effort to create and maintain.

Plan for activity areas and storage needs of each person in your household. Plan these arrangements as a group when others are sharing the materials. List the categories of materials and then list the storage furniture you want for each room, such as: bookshelves, storage cabinets, computer desks, file cabinets, desks or tables and wall units or entertainment systems.

Always plan for miscellaneous containers and storage space to hold odd items that don't fit any of your groups. For example, you might have a miscellaneous drawer in the kitchen and also in the bedroom and the bathroom. In other locations, a small basket or box works for collecting odds and ends. Reorganize these storage arrangements when your materials are growing too numerous for the current arrangement or containers.

Easy Categories to Organize

Kitchen supplies – Frequently used items located in front for convenience, less frequently used items located in back, and rarely used items located in long-term storage with labeled containers and managed with inventory lists.

Sports equipment – These are kept in storage bins in a closet or basement, unless the quantity is large enough to separate into groups and organize on shelving or inside cabinets.

Tools – Keep in one location or toolbox, with large quantities organized by categories or by usage patterns and stored on shelving or otherwise in suitable cabinets.

Clothes – Organize by the categories of options, such as school or work clothes, dressy clothes, better sportswear, and casual sportswear. Also may group by seasonal or each kind of item, such as: blue jeans, sweatshirts, polo shirts, t-shirts, etc.

Linen closets- These closets replace older style cedar chests used to store blankets and sheets, unless they get filled with sports equipment first. Then add an extra storage cabinet.

Neglected Categories to Organize

Paper collections – Financial papers and records are the most important categories to organize, and then practical information collections for your personal interests.

Books – Group by subject matter categories such as cooking, health, sports and fiction. For large quantities of books, also group by subtopics for better organization.

Office supplies – Your usage patterns and materials determine the arrangement and locations. High activity requires a separate cabinet or area, but low activity can share a storage cabinet.

Hobbies and collectibles- Plan the containers and convenient locations for collections. The biggest category today is CD's that can be organized by categories and stored on racks or in boxes.

Miscellaneous- Small baskets or decorative boxes are handy to store items that collect on desks, coffee tables, bedside tables and in bathrooms. Occasionally sort and put away these items when large quantities are collecting.

Many people use three kinds of storage areas shown below. Frequently used items are stored in more handy locations for convenience. Less frequently used items are stored further back out of the way, and rarely used items are stored in long-term storage areas. Boxes work well for storing papers and books, whereas sturdy large plastic bags take up less space for storing soft items like extra clothing and blankets.

Write inventory lists and label the containers, since it's easy to forget what items you have placed in long-term storage. Inventories help you keep track of large amounts of materials, and they help you manage better organization and restocking some items as necessary. You will find that inventory lists are essential if you're starting a small business or have complex patterns of activities and materials.

Three Levels of Storage

Frequently used items stored out in front for easy access, and organized by categories and usage patterns. Keep the materials handy in locations where they are being used.

Occasionally used items stored in back for less frequent use, with inventory lists for large quantities of items, especially if timely restocking of items is important.

Rarely used items store these materials out of the way for long-term storage, using labeled containers and inventory lists to keep track of large quantities of materials.

Organizing Paperwork

Paperwork tends to be the most disorganized category among our possessions, while the need to deal with complex paperwork is increasing. It seems automatic for people to organize their large possessions, while it seems equally automatic for people to neglect their paper collections. Papers tend to accumulate in random piles, making it difficult to find specific papers when you need them or even to remember the location of specific papers. Using fairly simple strategies to organize paperwork and storage can improve your level of efficiency, especially if you're dealing with numerous paperwork activities.

You always have paperwork at school, at work and at home that requires organization if you don't want to waste time. In every situation where your productivity depends upon efficiency with paperwork, good organization improves your functioning. When you're planning your educational activities, you don't want to waste time searching for papers in order to get paperwork done. So if you're spending an excessive amount of time on paperwork, you will soon realize the value of better organization for improving your efficiency with paperwork.

It's unnecessary to create elaborate systems for organizing paperwork, since simple organization usually works quite well. For activities at home, store papers in labeled manila envelopes or paper file folders. List the contents on top and put a label on the side edge to arrange them in file cabinets. Use rubber bands to group piles of bills that you want to save for several years, and it helps to add labels on top of the piles. You can save time and energy and get better results by the organizing paperwork for most of your activities at work, at school and at home.

Saving Information Collections

Information papers in disorganized piles tend to remain unused, whereas papers saved in organized storage are easily found and used for your thinking and activities. Arrange home information collections in categories such as health, home maintenance, travel, hobbies, recipes, etc. Manila envelopes and paper folders work great for simple information storage at home. Write a summary of contents on top of each envelope or folder so you can see at a glance what's inside each container.

When you begin sorting, you will find that information papers can be organized quickly. Use a sheet of paper to name each pile when sorting papers, so you can modify your pile names and divide large piles into subtopics. At the end of sorting, you will have refined groups and file names. Large piles can be divided into subtopics, and related files can be grouped into categories. Arrange individual papers in categories with the most recent ones placed first, unless you have found another arrangement that's more effective for your activities. At regular intervals it's worth sorting and discarding old papers, since information collections tend to become outdated. Occasionally update your collections by discarding old papers and adding new ones, and this takes much less time than might be expected.

The typical business filing system is very effective for large paper collections at home, but file cabinets are unnecessary. Store paper files in boxes or plastic bins of the right size, and add cardboard dividers labeled with bold titles to separate the categories. Arrange the manila envelopes and paper folders like regular files inside your boxes or desk drawers with titles written along the upper edge. You will be amazed how much this simple organization increases your efficiency.

Storing Financial Records
Financial records are often neglected piles of paper managed with wishful thinking that your budget will work out good enough without planning and organizing papers. It works better to keep track of financial activities with written records and organized paperwork. Begin with a complete summary or inventory of your financial activities and paperwork. List due dates when bills must be paid and organize paperwork by categories for storage.

Write inventories of financial activities and paperwork, so you can keep track of everything for comprehensive budget planning. For example, list all of your monthly bills in order of the due date when they must be paid, and use separate containers for each category of bills or expenses. Write summary sheets about your monthly and annual patterns of activity so you can keep track of all categories of financial activities for budget planning.

Manila envelopes make good storage containers for budget summaries, receipts, educational bills and for personal records. Place a title on top of each envelope and list a summary or inventory of the contents for easy reference. Also you might list the due dates for bills and checkmark items when they are paid. Examples of titles on your envelopes might be auto expenses, housing and utilities bills, food expenses, health expenses, and miscellaneous expenses.

Store financial papers in separate envelopes by categories, with a summary of activities on top each envelope. List the due dates of bills on a calendar page so you have a reminder. You can store manila envelopes in regular filing cabinets or in cardboard boxes of the right size. Complete this system with "in" and "out" boxes to hold your bills and papers until you can process them and place them in storage. Update your system occasionally by sorting out old papers that should be discarded or shredded, or otherwise placed in long-term storage.

Use separate envelopes for educational expenses and also for tax planning paperwork, with the contents summarized on top. At the end of each year, all of your relevant papers will be ready for processing taxes. Simply add copies of your finished tax forms to the envelope and put this away in storage when you're done. Good organization makes it easy to keep track of financial paperwork and to deal with financial planning.

Store your most important papers in a separate container that you can take along for an emergency evacuation. You need to find these papers quickly and take them along to conduct your business or lifestyle from another location. Save important records and budget sheets in a separate envelope, and also include summary lists for each category of papers. Keep copies of your most important papers and identification information stored in a secure location like a bank safety deposit box.

Computer accounting programs help manage complex budget planning and also small business records more efficiently. This kind of programming makes it easy to organize large quantities of information and print various summary sheets. Often financial paperwork at home is too simple to use computer programming for organizing your information and printing summary sheets. However if you decide to save financial information in computer files, make backup copies or print paper copies regularly so the information won't be lost when your computer malfunctions, since this can be expected occasionally.

Organizing Computer Study Notes

Easily collect classroom lecture notes by handwriting your notes in class, followed by recopying them into computer word files. You can use a fast scribble while concentrating on the message as you write notes by hand during class and also during reading. Then you can learn more from the process of recopying your notes into computer files while you check for good organization. Spiral notebooks are convenient for note writing by hand in class, but they lack flexibility for reorganizing them with your reading and thinking notes unless you recopy them.

Loose leaf paper provides more flexibility for reorganizing handwritten notes. These papers are easily reshuffled as much as you want since they're not fixed in place. The individual pages can be reorganized and recopied along with your thinking notes. You can mix these pages with unlined printer paper that's hole-punched for three-ring storage. Loose-leaf papers can be stored in paper folders for convenience, and when you're done using these notes, they can be stored in simple flat paper holders.

Computer word files provide more flexibility for study notes since these notes are easily reorganized and combined with your other computer note collections. Reorganizing these notes helps process the material with higher forms of analysis and synthesis. All of your reading and lecture notes can be reorganized and combined to provide more perspective for analysis. Any number of neat copies can be printed for thinking and review activities. Instead of struggling to read scribbled notes, you can easily skim your neat printed copies for an efficient review.

The most commonly used files today are computer word files, and these files are easily organized into groups and categories like paper files. Group related files into "computer folders" with group names, and these folders can be grouped with category and division names. When you open a folder, you won't need to sort through hundreds of file names. You simply open the right category and group name, and you will see a limited number of files to sort. Grouping your computer files into categories also provides some organizing perspective about your activities, and your specific files are always easy to find.

Secure important computer files with backup copies, or else the information will be lost when your computer malfunctions. Several forms of backup copies are possible. The easiest form of backup copy is simply printing out an updated paper copy occasionally. This copy can be scanned back into a computer or entered by hand if necessary. Another method of making backup copies is saving your files on external computer disks, and these forms can be updated by recopying them on the same disks. Always check your backup copies to be sure they are successful copies, so you can read and use them if necessary.

A common form of making backup copies consists of saving copies on CD's or DVD's, since these hold enough data for most purposes. However these forms cannot be rewritten over unless the discs are designated as having that capacity. If you use CD's or DVD's that can be rewritten over, then you can save updated files over the top of old files. These copies are more efficient than paper for large quantities of data, but CD's typically have a fairly short life span of only a few years. The newest device for back-up copies consists of small "flash drives", also called thumb drives. These devices plug into recent computer models, and they last longer and hold larger quantities of data.

Inventory Your Complex Patterns
Inventories are simply lists organized by topics and categories. They are powerful tools for organization and complex planning. Unless you have a very simple lifestyle, it's difficult to function well without written lists and inventories. Written records and

inventories are essential for businesses that must manage very large quantities of information and materials. Your efficiency of functioning with many ordinary everyday activities is also greatly increased with these records, and it only takes a few minutes to create these simple lists for written records.

Lists and inventories are your tools for keeping track of large quantities of materials easily and complex patterns of activities. Long-term storage items in your attic are difficult to find and use unless you have written inventories. People with gigantic closets might need an inventory list to plan what to wear. If you have large quantities of movies on DVD's, take an inventory list shopping so you don't buy duplicates. If you read recipe books, you won't remember many recipes unless you write inventory lists with descriptive names, the title of the book and the page number. Use your inventory lists during menu planning to plan for healthy menus and write a shopping list.

Written lists and inventories provide a roadmap for efficient functioning by helping organize and coordinate large quantities of information and materials. Written records about planning, information and materials create summaries for managing very complex activities or a busy lifestyle. Create inventory lists for materials and even activities, so your summaries and planning lists provide a complete picture for functioning. Inventory lists work like a table of contents for large collections of information and paperwork. They help you manage very large quantities of information, activities and materials efficiently.

Getting Organized Mentally
People tend to have about seven issues in mind at any one time, it has been said. You can become better organized mentally by listing your current concerns, so your attention and focus can be distributed efficiently upon your strongest priorities. Even if you can't find seven issues, it's good to clarify what you're working on mentally, using both speech and writing to clarify thinking. Organizing and writing ideas helps you think more efficiently, so you can continue building and developing your ideas.

Your greatest organizational needs in the future will consist of managing knowledge and paperwork rather than dealing with material things. It's likely you will be managing more paperwork and information than most people had to deal with in the past. You may find yourself often searching for information, and then collecting and organizing information for your various activities and concerns. Your knowledge needs are growing similar to the requirements for business, so your most effective functioning depends upon using better strategies to deal with information and to plan your activities.

You will tend to acquire knowledge lifelong for many kinds of activities and interests, so you can benefit significantly by using excellent strategies for organizing and processing knowledge. Increase your efficiency with learning and with practical activities by using note writing for processing knowledge. Your basic tools for managing knowledge consist of note writing skills for reading and planning writing, for gathering and organizing knowledge for your thinking and for problem solving for practical applications. Use strategies from the previous chapters to process knowledge efficiently for your many activities and applications.

ORGANIZING TIME

Your Limited Resource
"Don't waste time" is a popular expression. Regardless of good intentions, following this advice is practically impossible unless you're planning goals and scheduling time. First you must decide what to do each day, or randomly think of worthwhile things to do each day. Since you're either going to school or to work most of the time, these activities provide something worthwhile to do. The bulk of your time is scheduled for you in the workplace and also during the lower levels of education.

Your study activities and recreation options are not scheduled for you during higher education. So it's your own responsibility entirely to plan for activities and to schedule study time. You will have many options for activities, so writing a schedule helps to ensure that you are planning enough time to finish study goals and also participate in preferred recreation activities.

"Time is your most limited resource" is another popular expression, and therefore time must be carefully managed to reach many achievement goals. You may discover too late that inadequate time management limits achievement. Poor quality time management is the biggest stumbling block for adequate achievement in higher education. You can be certain of reaching your educational goals by listing weekly and daily planning for study activities and then by scheduling enough time.

Students require time management for high achievement. Time scheduling translates goals are into action, so that planning becomes more than a vague passing thought. Time scheduling is essential when you want to be certain about reaching your goals, and you want to be certain that your work is getting done on time instead of being delayed because of some procrastination. Planning study goals and scheduling time is essential for greater achievement with your education.

Coordinate Planning and Scheduling

Time management begins with writing planning lists about your most important categories of activities. Organize separate lists for each topic of planning, so it's easier to keep track of your numerous activities and concerns. Your level of achievement in many categories, especially in higher education, depends upon organizing activities with planning and then scheduling time.

The common time units of annual, monthly, weekly and daily are handy to organize your scheduling, since it's convenient to schedule activities in these time units. At the beginning of each year, take some time to review your annual planning categories. Instead of simply choosing some New Year's resolutions, use this opportunity to review long-term goals. At the beginning of each month, take time to review planning for short-term activities and write weekly schedules. It's more efficient to plan short-term activities in terms of monthly and weekly time units, and then you can simply update your daily lists as you go along.

Simple scheduling consists of writing occasional activities in the daily spaces on a calendar, and this might be combined with daily lists or reminders. Otherwise at the beginning of each week or day, write your "to-do list" of activities for that day or week. You can add time suggestions alongside your listed activities or else transfer your list onto a time schedule if you have many items to complete. When you have only a few activities on your list, writing a simple "to do list" works fine.

You might prefer using a weekly grid schedule that shows all of your waking hours for each week. Also write lists of weekly activities by categories or topics, and organize the total workload you want to finish each week and day. Keep track of progress for your workload with checklists, so you can adjust your pace to finish your scheduled work on time. You might check mark the priority work items when you're finished.

A popular schedule minder for the workplace is a notebook with a separate page for scheduling each day, or else you might use a computer version of this schedule minder. First list your activities by topics, then use a scheduling notebook to organize your time. Calendar pages are useful to keep track of important dates, and use "post-it" notes for the exceptions and reminders. Use small notebooks to carry around for collecting ideas and planning activity lists. After scheduling study activities, you can see how much time is left for optional activities.

Today, students are most likely placing their schedules into computer organizers and printing copies of different views, such as monthly, weekly and daily. Consider what kinds of scheduling tools can best meet your need to keep track of activities.

Steps for Choosing Scheduling Tools

* Use calendar pages for reminders about important dates

* Use large and small "post-it" notes for simple "to-do lists" and extra reminders

* Small spiral notebooks are handy for collecting lists of ideas and writing planning lists

* Students might use an hourly grid for the week with space to schedule all of their activities for the week

* Career workers prefer a daily planner notebook that contains a separate page to schedule each day

* Consider a computer scheduler that can print different views

Using combinations of time management tools works better for complex patterns of activity. Try separate lists and schedules for some different categories of activities. This insures that one schedule doesn't become too cluttered for easy reference. Separate schedules work best for projects that require frequent reminders, so you can keep checking on these often. When using separate schedules for different activities, also place all of your items onto one combined schedule. Sometimes you need to design your own scheduling tools to show what helps you keep track of complex or unusual patterns of activity.

Using A Weekly Grid Schedule

Students manage time better by using a weekly grid schedule that shows all of their daytime hours on one page for each week. This kind of schedule helps you keep track of the total time available during the week for study versus for other activities. This schedule promotes awareness about your distribution of work, so you can be certain that time isn't being wasted when you have many activities on your planning list.

Prepare enough weekly grid pages for several months or the whole semester so you can also schedule long-term assignments such as research papers. First prepare one grid page showing all of your "fixed items" during the week, such as meals, sleeping time, commuting and scheduled classes. Photocopy enough pages for each week in the semester. Write in estimated study time for each class, for long-term projects and priority goals. Then add the optional activities from your planning lists.

Always use separate planning lists along with any schedule, since this makes it easier to keep track of your priority activities. List all work activities that you want to finish each week, also organize lists showing the work you want to finish each day.

Write your study sessions on the hourly grid schedule first, before adding optional items. Write in work goals for each day and study session, balanced with rest breaks. You might check mark the work done on your lists if this helps you keep track of finishing priority work or adjusting your pace.

A weekly grid schedule provides wide perspective about your total activities and time usage for the week. You can write this kind of schedule with a computer organizer that shows different views, so you can look at a day, a week or month at a time and print copies of different views. The weekly grid schedule provides the wide perspective required to budget time wisely. Use this schedule with flexibility to plan for a reasonable balance of activities. You still need small notebooks for collecting ideas and planning lists. Add calendar pages to keep track of occasional events, and use "post-it" notes for extra reminders.

Scheduling Study Goals

Scheduling time periods for study often results in rest periods with very little studying getting done. It works better to set work goals for each session and day, and then check mark work that's finished off your list. This should help you keep track of finishing enough work during each day and week.

Study sessions without work goals are less effective because you might not work diligently enough if you haven't set specific time goals. When you list and schedule your workload, you may realize that you don't have enough time for high quality study. This realization begins to grow when you list your total workload and distribute the items on your time schedule. Then you need to choose priorities so you can be certain about finishing the most important study activities on your list.

Distribute your total study workload for each week and day among your available time sessions. Hopefully there's enough free time left if you need extra study time. Since you can only estimate the time required for study each day, if your work isn't finished, use time from optional activities. If your scheduled time is inadequate for listed work goals, adjust your schedule to use time from lower priority activities or else adjust your work pace. Then finally consider reducing your workload.

Listing and scheduling your total workload helps to insure that enough work is getting done within the recommended time. Otherwise you will be amazed how quickly time disappears without getting much work done. Then you might wonder what's the secret to high achievement. The secret is keeping track of your workload, time schedule and the items of work finished, so that your time is being used effectively. The following steps are useful to help you manage time.

Steps for Scheduling Study

* List your total workload for each week and day

* Distribute your workload among daily study sessions

* Set work goals for each day and each study session

* Check mark the work finished off your list or schedule

* Schedule sessions for long-term projects and review

Schedule study with realistic expectations about time that's required for achieving your goals. It's not realistic to expect expert level learning from only one course of study that lasts a few months and that covers only one textbook. Long-term study is required for higher levels of achievement. If you prefer to study thoroughly for difficult subjects, or if your achievement goals are very high, it's better to take a reduced workload in order to have more study time. Reasonable expectations help you manage time and energy more efficiently.

Scheduling Steps of Complex Activities

If you're afraid you can't do highly complex tasks, you're right. Complex activity is only manageable by breaking it down into steps and sequencing the steps, so that you're doing each step easily. This is similar to mathematical problems that must be solved as a series of logical steps being done in the right order. Usually complex activities must be done one step at a time, and in the right order, and then each of these steps is easy enough to perform and coordinate into the whole task. Sometimes you may be unaware of performing some tasks as separate steps.

Often work that seems simple must be separated into steps or you'll run into difficulty with the whole process. For example, if you're painting a room in your house, you must break it down into separate steps and schedule them. Usually the first step is preparing the surface by cleaning. Then sanding and patching may be required, followed by priming the patches. Next prepare the painting area with masking tape and drop cloths, and finally you can paint. You must estimate the amount of time for each separate step and then schedule a suitable time that doesn't conflict with your other routine or scheduled activities.

When writing a research paper, don't simply schedule writing. Instead schedule the steps you're using for writing the paper. The first step is organizing your current ideas and information into a preliminary plan. The next step is research reading and taking notes. Then organize a writing plan for the length of your paper. The next step is writing the first draft of your paragraphs.

Finally, add one or more days for revisions, and then you can print out a final copy. Several sessions may be necessary to complete each of these steps for long papers. Since you can only estimate the time required for each step of large projects, allow some extra time for unexpected delays.

Try to schedule separate sessions for the individual steps of difficult and complex tasks. For example if you want to design a complex machine for your research project, you must perform various activities and in the right order. First you must plan the general functioning of the machine and then plan subsystems, coordinating the functioning among subsystems. Then you must build and test the machine. Finally you must prepare written instructions for the users. It's easy to see the value of separate steps for complex activities. It's equally easy to overlook the need for separate steps when your activities are fairly simple, but they still can't be done properly as one single step.

Leaving Some Free Time
It's wise to leave some time for rest, recreation, social events and thinking in your schedule. Consider planning for pleasant rest breaks or a change of activity between long study sessions. Continuous study doesn't promote your best quality of learning, so arrange for reasonable rest-breaks. You can learn better with small rest breaks between small study goals and with longer rest breaks between longer study sessions. Otherwise you might take random rest breaks that waste too much time, and you might fail to achieve your important study goals.

Good rest breaks from study are going for a walk, getting a drink or nap, and discussion with others. Other good rest breaks are social activities and physical exercises that can improve your circulation and mental energy. Small rest breaks within sessions don't need to be written since it adds clutter to your schedule. Longer rest-breaks might be planned and written on your schedule as a change of activity. Some students find it helpful to take a break every hour or half hour. They might do stretching exercises, walk around for awhile and get a drink, or else just lean back and think about the material.

Consider scheduling difficult work for your high energy time of the day. This means early in the day if you work better in the morning. Schedule easier work and social activities for later when you're tired and will have lower concentration. Avoid doing very challenging work in the late evening hours and during party nights at your location, with only rare exceptions. You can improve upon educational achievement by listing your goals and activities, and then by scheduling the most effective use of your time and energy.

When you want more time for high priority goals, use some time from optional activities. Your extra time is found wherever lower priority activities are scheduled. Otherwise you might consider working faster and in more efficient ways. If these measures are inadequate, try reducing your workload to achieve priority goals. Time scheduling increases your awareness about how time is being used, so you can plan for balanced activities and keeping track of priorities while including some recreation. It's unnecessary to fill all the spaces on your schedule, but try to use enough time scheduling to provide reasonable assurance that you can finish your priority study activities.

Good study opportunities are more likely to be lost from lack of planning than from noisy roommates. If you must adapt to unusual circumstances in your living quarters, then schedule for the situation. Try to get cooperation from your roommates with some scheduling. Use group discussion to identify and agree upon time scheduling for study versus recreation and rest. Then you will have the same free time for group activities, so you can coordinate some planning for recreation.

ORGANIZING EVALUATION

A Continuous Process
Your continual state of learning and change is the weak link for planning and scheduling. Throughout your life you will continue adding new information and ideas, and this tends to change your outlook and interests for planning. For business planning, there's a continuous and ongoing need to keep up with new information and changes in the marketplace. Managers must try to keep up-to-date with relevant developments for their business interests, and use planning to accommodate the changes going on around them in the market for their products or services.

Instead of making plans and sticking with them forever, it's better to reconsider your planning and progress occasionally and to seek improvements over time. Otherwise your planning may become outdated, you may toss it out, and that's the end of planning. The process of planning is renewed with evaluation. This means thinking about changes in your life, your interests, your knowledge and degree of progress so you can consider the need for updating and revising your planning.

The process of evaluation tends to be continuous and ongoing for all complex activities, and even for many ordinary activities. Even on an informal level, you will find that people are often reconsidering how well their achievement activities are working in order to make adjustments in their functioning. This can be done more effectively on a conscious level and with written lists and records that help you keep track of your ideas and progress, especially for complex activities. Evaluation is an important step for tracking progress and improving planning.

Evaluation is a tool for developing better planning over time, and this step is performed with your annual review of planning. This step consists of evaluating new information and ideas that you have collected, thinking about the changes around you and your level of progress. Consider that many aspects of life around you might be changing, and that continuous learning and change might affect your outlook. Occasionally it's wise to reconsider if the changes in your circumstances and outlook are creating a need for revising your planning. You will find that evaluation is the best tool for improving planning over time. The following steps are useful to guide the process of evaluation.

Steps to Evaluate Planning

1) Evaluate new ideas and information to update planning

2) Review your progress and reconsider planning by categories

3) Consider revising and improving upon planning with your new information and ideas

Coordinating Your Own System

Gain greater educational efficiency and find your direction in life by identifying your priorities and managing your achievement with planning and scheduling. Planning is the most important step for becoming organized and increasing your achievement. Begin by identifying all categories of your interests and choosing personal goals. List your ideas for planning, then occasionally review your planning so you can maintain adequate focus and balance on your most important concerns.

Coordinate your own system for improving both knowledge and planning over time by organizing information collections and maintaining adequate written records. Collecting and organizing information about your interests helps you continually improve upon the quality of your planning. Save organized collections of information and coordinate them with planning categories to build knowledge for improved functioning. Organize and analyze information collections with note writing, and you can improve your quality of planning and functioning over time.

Organization is the fundamental underlying strategy for all forms of highly effective functioning. List, analyze and organize everything you want planned and managed for important goals. Process knowledge with organizational strategies that help you reach greater levels of achievement with learning and practical activities. Maintain organized records and materials that increase your productivity. Choose suitable scheduling tools to organize time for your activities. You can significantly improve your level of achievement and quality of everyday functioning by using adequate organizational strategies for planning and scheduling the activities required to achieve your goals.

Planning, organizing, scheduling and evaluating are the basic steps used for organizing productivity in business. These steps provide the most comprehensive system for managing personal achievement activities as effectively as a business. Although personal planning is much less complex than business planning, these four steps are uniquely effective for managing all forms of achievement, both simple and complex. These four business steps provide an efficient and ongoing process for identifying your options and interests and dealing with changes that may affect your planning. These four steps are equally effective for managing your short-term educational achievement goals and for managing your progress towards long-term goals.

Quick Steps for Organization

Choose your topics and categories for planning

List your current planning ideas for each category

List long-term goals and priority items to maintain focus

List your short-term goals and schedule weekly activities

Collect information to improve upon complex planning

Organize materials and information for your activities

Choose scheduling tools to organize time for activities

4 HOME STUDY AND TEACHING

Learning and Teaching Steps

OUTLINE CONTENT of knowledge and learning skills practice for a study course

CHOOSE TECHNIQUES and methods for teaching and learning

SCHEDULE TIME to cover the knowledge content and practice with learning and practical skills

SUMMARY PLANNING in the teachers plan book or as the syllabus for higher education

DAILY PLANNING in greater detail to implement your summary planning

PROBLEMS OF LEARNING/TEACHING

You can't learn everything in school that you want to learn, so you should know how to plan for good quality study at home. Regardless of what you're studying in school, you may find deficiencies with your knowledge and learning skills or you might simply wish to learn more. The summary steps in this chapter for planning teaching and learning can help you organize better home study and home schooling or tutoring for others.

Everyone needs good strategies for studying and teaching since these subjects are highly interrelated. Teachers should know how to teach all of the study strategies and learning skills. Lesson planning by teachers should provide practice with basic learning skills so students are improving in these important skills while gaining knowledge. Both high school and college students should know what to expect from a teacher's lesson planning. When students understand how a course of study is organized, and what kinds of assignments and study skills are expected of them, they can achieve their learning goals efficiently.

The definition of an educated person is changing from simply doing reading, writing and arithmetic to gaining a foundation of knowledge and learning skills to continue with lifelong learning. The goal of education consists of gaining suitable knowledge content, such as covering the subject matter we value learning. Education goals also consist of gaining adequate learning skills for your best functioning. You should develop greater skills with reading, writing, speaking, listening and thinking, while you should be developing research skills for continued learning.

Good quality study at home and teaching begins with planning for adequate knowledge content and practice with suitable learning skills that meet functioning goals. This chapter presents basic summary steps for planning teaching, and also explains how to use these steps for planning better quality learning at home.

In the past, teaching largely consisted of common routines. The common teaching routine for elementary levels was "just work through the books" for each subject matter, doing reading, writing, verbal and practical activities that reinforce learning the material. The common teaching routine for the high school and college levels consisted of lecture and discussion in class, with homework of assigned reading and written work that might include a research paper. Also two tests were required, a mid-term and a final exam. Student grades were based on tests and written papers, and to some extent on student attendance and participation. Although it's difficult to change these common procedures, by analyzing the activities we can use for teaching and learning it's possible to make worthwhile improvements.

Analyzing learning and teaching begins with listing all of the activities we can use for studying, learning and teaching. These are all of the techniques we can use to deal with knowledge and learning, and we get a list like the following:

reading, writing, listening, speaking, thinking, doing things and watching others doing things

In other words, the list of activities for learning is reading and related tasks, writing and related tasks, listening, speaking and discussion, and also practical activities or demonstrations. An important part of study activities is that we learn from thinking that accompanies all of these other activities. These activities represent learning skills students must practice to continue intellectual growth, and the activities also match the categories of teaching techniques in the list below (McKeachie 123, 307). Two more categories are added here to emphasize study skills and teaching methods, often neglected in planning teaching.

CATEGORIES OF TEACHING TECHNIQUES

Reading – Assign reading about the study content from various sources such as books, magazines, newspapers, workbooks, handout sheets and the content on computer web sites.

Written Work - Assign practice with various forms of writing such as outlines and summaries, research reports, essays, creative writing and journal entries. Assign practice writing notes to learn from reading, speaking, listening, planning writing and also to learn from many practical activities and demonstrations. Students may write questions for discussion and quizzes.

Verbal Activity – Provide opportunities for listening, speaking and group discussion. Use activities such as lecture, questioning, explanation, student verbal reports, buzz groups, verbal quizzes, recordings, interviews, guest speakers, debates, reviewing and brainstorming sessions as a group.

Practical Application – Use practical activities suitable to reinforce learning from reading. Popular items include lab work science experiments, games, role-playing, guest presentations, bulletin boards, interest centers, picture displays, films, slide shows, overhead projector displays, field trips, demonstrations, TV programs and computer learning exercises.

NEGLECTED CATEGORIES FOR PLANNING TEACHING

Study Skills – Plan assignments that provide balanced practice with key skills: reading, writing, thinking, speaking and listening. Assign practice with writing study notes from reading, such as outlines, summaries and other notes for analysis of material. Assign practice writing notes to plan for speaking and written papers. Upper level students need practice with note writing for higher levels of thinking and practice with writing various written papers such as essays and research papers.

Methods of Teaching – Use summaries at the end of this section to choose methods for conducting classroom activities. Methods of teaching are organized into the following categories: Information Processing Models, Social Interaction Models, Personal Learning Models and Behavioral Systems Models.

Write Summary Planning
Problems in planning teaching are found at all educational levels from elementary through college. Elementary teaching textbooks focus on daily lesson planning, neglecting summary planning for the long-term view. As time goes by, the daily planning doesn't make enough sense because it lacks comprehensive organization in terms of the whole year or semester.

In contrast, college teaching textbooks focus upon summary planning or the "syllabus" for the whole semester or whole year. Daily lesson planning lacks variety in college, consisting mainly of lecture and discussion. You can improve upon planning by combining strategies from the various levels of teaching.

Write summary planning first for a whole semester or year before writing daily planning. Use the steps for planning teaching and the techniques and methods for teaching to write long-term summary planning. Use the format below to write the syllabus summaries for higher level courses. And use the other format to organize daily planning for elementary lessons.

Summary planning for the whole year should cover the best choice of content and learning activities for the course goals. Summary planning should include activities from all categories of teaching techniques, and include suitable methods for teaching. Good quality lesson planning provides suitable activities that can increase both knowledge and learning skills for students.

Similar formats are being used to organize summary planning for elementary lesson planning and for the upper level syllabus. Listed below are examples of these planning formats.

Elementary Lesson Plan	Study Course Syllabus
Time Scheduled for Subject	Schedule of Subtopics
Content Outline and Goals	Books and Materials
Books and Materials	Extra Collateral Reading
Assignments and Homework	Assignments and Test Dates
Methods and Procedures	Class Special Activity Days
Evaluation and Testing	Student Responsibilities

Begin summary planning with your school curriculum guide and the materials provided such as textbooks and time schedule. Then use the teaching techniques, the teaching methods, and the planning formats like those listed above. You might add or delete categories according to your requirements and goals for the course of study. Consider including a category for computer activities, since students are using computers for learning today. Plan for balanced practice with knowledge and learning skills and for practice with relevant practical skills.

STEPS TO PLAN TEACHING/LEARNING

1) Outline knowledge content topics and list the practice activities for learning skills and practical skills

List your study course goals in terms of knowledge content, practice with learning skills, practical skills, and even improved attitudes. Use your school curriculum guide and the materials provided to briefly outline the subject matter. Evaluate current learning goals and gather additional materials as necessary.

List assignments and activities, using all categories of the teaching techniques below. First choose reading assignments. Then add written activities, verbal and practical activities that reinforce learning from the reading material.

Identify the written work and testing to be used for grading, and what levels of performance to use for grading categories. See the section about written work for easy grading categories.

2) Choose the teaching techniques and teaching methods to use for knowledge content and skills practice

READING- List books, materials and reading assignments, and list the dates when assignments are scheduled.

WRITTEN WORK- List suitable written work and testing. List separate written activities for the classroom versus homework assignments. Identify what written activities will be used for evaluation and what standards will be used for grading.

VERBAL ACTIVITY- Choose verbal activities for teaching the knowledge content in class, while providing practice with the skills of listening and speaking. List the topics for lecture or explanation, discussion, review, and for reciting or reports.

PRACTICAL APPLICATIONS AND SKILLS- List the practical activities or demonstrations, lab experiments, role-playing and miscellaneous classroom activities and materials that enhance interest in learning the subject matter.

STUDY SKILLS- Choose practical study skill activities for the content and grade level so students are developing adequate skills with reading, writing, thinking, speaking and listening.

METHODS OF TEACHING- Use summaries at the end of this section to choose suitable teaching methods or procedures for the subject matter and level of instruction.

3) Time schedule distribution of content and activities

Distribute a brief outline of topics into the time schedule for the whole year or semester. Then distribute the reading and writing assignments and written test dates. Schedule additional assignments, quizzes and verbal activities to enhance learning from reading and writing. Adjust quantity of work for the time schedule, and allow flexibility in the amount of work for each session, since time usage can only be estimated.

Schedule the best use of time to cover knowledge content and practice with basic learning skills, so that time is being used efficiently to meet the study course goals. In this step, you can separate work that's scheduled for classroom activities versus for homework. Prepare handout sheets for students, listing the homework along with the time schedule. This helps students plan their study schedule at home, and it helps parents who may need to monitor some students.

4) Write summary planning in the teacher's plan book, or write a syllabus for the higher levels of education

Write a record of your summary planning for each semester of the study course. Then outline your summary planning in the syllabus, or the teacher's plan book for lower levels of education, adding extra pages if necessary. Include adequate information in your plan book for a substitute teacher, so it won't be necessary for the substitute to create new planning or else to simply use some review for each subject matter time period.

The elementary teacher's plan book only has room for brief descriptions of planned activities for each class session, so add separate planning lists to fully describe your summary planning for each subject matter during the semester. Begin summary planning by listing what subject matter topics will be covered during each week and day, and what time periods are being devoted to each subject daily. Listed below are the typical subjects being taught, along with the estimated time schedule that might be used for elementary levels of teaching.

Subject Matter	Minutes Daily
Reading	60
Mathematics	40
Language Arts, Writing Spelling, Penmanship	40
Science	40
Social Studies	40
Physical Education	30
Art, Music	30

Elementary teachers plan all these subjects each semester, except that some schools use teaching specialists for music and physical education. High school and college teachers only plan one subject matter, repeated during their classes each day. Lower level schools provide a curriculum guide along with the textbooks and time schedule for each level of instruction. Your curriculum guide might contain adequate information to organize summary planning for each semester or school year.

Upper level students during high school and college should get copies of a course syllabus at the beginning of their classes. The syllabus is a course outline, showing the schedule of study topics and the reading and writing assignments and tests. Also it lists the books and materials being used, when the assignments are due, and the dates for testing. This helps students plan their schedules and prepare for class activities and testing. A syllabus or course summary can be reused with only annual updates. Prepare a seating chart within the first few days of class so you can learn the students' names and check attendance daily.

5) Outline daily planning in greater detail to implement your summary planning

Write daily lesson planning in an outline form when you don't need highly detailed planning. An outline pattern provides some flexibility for adjusting the quantity of material and activities covered in a class session. Choose relevant category headings to organize daily planning. Briefly outline the knowledge content and list activities to provide practice with learning skills.

Outline your material for speaking and list useful activities to enhance learning. Plan your lecture and discussion topics for upper level education and plan classroom activities to reinforce knowledge content. Write detailed outlines for speaking when it's important to have the details organized accurately. Prepare fully written out content when you're teaching very complex subject matter that must be expressed precisely. See the section about speaking to prepare effective material for teaching.

Elementary teachers need two kinds of basic record books. One has attendance records and grades on tests and samples of academic work. Also save these graded papers to show parents at conferences, while you explain any academic weaknesses and behavior issues that may require additional practice at home. The teacher's plan book should contain the seating chart and summaries of daily lesson plans. It might include extra papers if detailed planning is required for some days. This should provide enough information for a substitute teacher when necessary.

ISSUES FOR HOME STUDY AND TEACHING

Evaluating Textbooks and Written Materials
You must evaluate the quality of books and written materials when you're planning teaching or home study. Your books and materials might be outdated or inadequate to meet the current learning goals. Evaluating textbooks is done fairly often for college level courses. The teacher surveys new textbooks and written materials in the subject matter area to find the best content available for current course goals. Sometimes this is required for the lower levels too, except these textbook options are limited since textbooks tend to be selected infrequently by school administrators or groups of experienced teachers.

When students just "work through the books" their education is deficient if these books lack suitable quality and content for current learning goals. Older textbooks might fail to cover the knowledge content in an adequate form to meet the new goals. Supplementary materials might not be available to provide some variety with student activities for their learning skills practice. Then teachers have the task of seeking additional materials, and these might be impossible to find for the lower levels. So the class proceeds with poor quality materials, and both the teacher and students may be blamed for poor quality results.

Teachers are expected to supplement the knowledge content when textbooks are inadequate. They can improve the course of study by adding content verbally in class and by providing extra reading materials. Even students can contribute to the course content by researching and reporting to the class what they have discovered about their study topics. Today, teachers have the opportunity to search online for additional content and lesson planning ideas that can be used to supplement outdated or inadequate textbooks and materials. Most teachers are adding supplementary materials in class occasionally, and the students tend to show great interest in this extra material.

Knowledge content is the most important consideration when planning upper-level study courses. Teachers simply try to find the best books and knowledge content available for their subject matter and level, and then design their own assignments and class activities for the course. They might seek supplementary materials or create them to enhance their classroom activities. Teachers might evaluate the quality of their current curriculum and the textbooks being used. If textbooks are poor quality, the students can share stories and inventory personal knowledge, also research for more information to share with the class.

Typically too much is expected of elementary level teachers in terms of improving a course of study. Teachers can't expect to find good textbooks and materials for the lower levels unless they have been specifically designed and created by experts. Currently there appears to be a lack of consistency in standards for curriculum and materials that are required for lower levels. Consequently lower level textbooks and materials are often inadequate, and teachers are expected to improvise. It's very difficult to improvise sufficiently to compensate for the lack of excellent materials for the lower levels of education. Generally you will need to use adult level materials and adapt them for your grade level and curriculum guidelines.

Uniform curriculum standards are important for lower levels of education. A core knowledge program of curriculum standards has been created for the elementary levels, and it's available online for teachers and experts to use as a guide in planning the educational content. It should be used to indicate what content to teach, and it should not be used to force students to perform at the same level. Also, the school curriculum should prepare students for testing requirements. Curriculum goals may include preparation for proficiency testing to pass the grade levels and also for future testing, such as the SAT and ACT that are used for college entrance. Students need experience with studying all categories of material required for their achievement testing.

Ideally experts should design all written materials and lesson planning for lower levels of education. The quality of curriculum materials shouldn't be left to beginning teachers who lack the resources and preparation for dealing with this kind of planning. For high quality teaching at lower levels of education, experts should plan for the appropriate knowledge content, materials and activities. Experts should plan the curriculum, design the books and the supplementary materials, and even provide daily lesson plans for teachers. Also these materials should be flexible and adaptable, since individual classes or students may learn at somewhat different levels and rates.

Planning for Student Accountability
You can hold students accountable for adequate achievement by assigning written work that corresponds to their non-written activities and then by grading the written work. For example if you simply assign reading, many students won't read and will waste time. If you assign written work based on their reading, students must read or it shows when grading their written work. Likewise for verbal activity, many students won't pay attention or participate unless they must write a summary or an essay after the verbal activity. Assign written work that shows if the

students are participating and reaching the learning goals being promoted by their non-written activities. Students need to show understanding of the key concepts in study material, and they should be able to discuss the material and write an essay.

In order to earn good grades, students must complete written assignments and demonstrate good levels of achievement with their written work. This form of accountability is equally useful for grading higher and lower level students. Use various forms of written work, such as different kinds of study notes and small quizzes and essays in class about the reading and discussion. Students can write summaries and outlines about their class discussions. They can write questions to quiz each other, also write and present verbal reports about their reading.

Assign some written work and essays as classroom activities so students can't cheat by copying or by having others do their written work. When students must write essays, small quizzes and other written work in class about study material, then it shows if the students are doing their own reading, thinking and listening. Inform students about these accountability measures and the learning goals in your introduction to the course. Explain the grading standards because it helps students keep their focus on working toward personal goals for good grades.

Formal tests aren't available for many learning activities, so written work is essential to provide evidence of the students' achievement. Written work is a stronger basis for grading than only testing, since it reveals more about the total quantity and quality of a student's achievement. Then graded written work and test scores can be added into the student's grade.

Students in upper level courses should have a course outline or syllabus to help manage study time and accountability goals. The course syllabus should list all assignments, activities, tests and due dates for written work. The assignments should include a list of homework along with the course outline and it should include the due dates for work during the whole semester.

Students plan their home study schedules more efficiently when homework is assigned on a long-term basis. Parents can use homework lists to check on the quality of work being done by students who may need monitoring. For lower level classes, the teacher might hand out a sheet of homework listed for the whole semester, or else post a weekly schedule in the classroom and discuss the achievement goals with students.

Some students don't function well unless the teacher pays attention to them as individuals. They may lack good behavior and academic performance unless the teacher notices and even provides suitable encouragement for them as individuals. Try to keep all your comments as positive as possible.

Using Teaching Techniques

The categories of teaching techniques are fundamental activities that promote balanced learning skills when they are used wisely for each level of education. Learning skills are promoted by the activities of reading, writing, listening, speaking, thinking and doing practical activities. Students learn more effectively when these various kinds of teaching techniques are used with their reading and writing activities. The students' intellectual growth depends on developing higher levels of learning skills that should be continually improving with practice.

Excellent lesson planning should provide balanced activities that promote the basic learning skills. Lesson planning should include assignments that build reading and writing skills, and it should include speaking and listening activities that promote improvement in these skills. Regardless of a teacher's speaking talent when presenting classroom lessons, students' education is deficient when they lack suitable assignments and activities for balanced practice with the basic learning skills.

The lesson planning examples in elementary teaching books often show classroom instruction as verbal activity exclusively, lacking in sufficient class time to practice reading and writing. This focus on verbal activity results in poor quality reading and writing skills, and especially for the lower levels of education. Students at lower levels need time for reading and writing, in addition to experience with all variations of learning techniques in order to develop balanced learning skills.

Lower level students learn better with a variety of activities during each day, and also during long class sessions. Variety increases student interest and it provides practice with additional skills. Students benefit from guided instruction in the classroom, showing them how to correctly perform some of the study skills. All levels of lesson planning should include activities promoting greater development of balanced learning skills.

Upper level classroom instruction tends is lacking variety and consists of lecture and discussion almost exclusively. Typically, upper levels of education require more attention to knowledge content, and this means an emphasis on techniques such as lecture and discussion that enables the teacher to share subject matter expertise. Typically the teacher adds more subject matter content in class if reading assignments focus on one textbook. However upper level students also require activities to practice higher level thinking and writing skills, since these students are expected to gain the higher levels of functioning.

Guided learning activities in class are beneficial for students at all educational levels, since many students don't learn as well doing assignments only by themselves. For example, high school students might read a poem in class and then write their own interpretation to share with discussion. When learning activities are done together as a group, this has the effect of "tutoring". Some guided classroom activity works better than having the students responsible for all their own learning from homework. Both the functioning level of the class and complexity of study material are useful to estimate what kinds of guided classroom activities can best improve learning for the class.

Variety is like spice that increases the students' interest and motivation for learning, even at the highest levels. Although it's important for students to have a variety of learning experiences, less variety is required as the school levels increase. Upper level students require greater focus upon knowledge content, while lower level students require more focus on basic learning skills. For all levels of students, it's wise to plan various class activities, using all four categories of the teaching techniques, since this stimulates interest and promotes balanced skills.

All the teaching techniques can be used with various teaching methods. The most common teaching methods used for all levels of education are "Direct Instruction" and "Advance Organizer". Generally these lessons have four stages of instruction. First, introduce the lesson by summarizing the concepts and learning goals. Second, present organized material and emphasize the organizing topics or "advance organizers". Third, assign reading, written work and supplementary activities to reinforce the study material and to provide learning skills practice. Fourth, conclude the lesson by summarizing the organizing topics.

Practicing Study Skills
Lesson planning may lack focus upon practicing learning skills and using the various kinds of methods for teaching. These two categories have been added to the teaching techniques in this chapter to call attention to the importance of planning for these concerns. The typical examples of lesson planning cover four categories of teaching techniques, which are reading, writing, verbal activity and practical applications. Although these basic skills are considered an intrinsic part of all teaching techniques, lesson planning should include focused attention upon adequate learning skills throughout the educational levels.

Lower level students need adequate practice with basic skills such as reading, writing, listening, speaking and thinking, while obtaining the appropriate knowledge content. Students require practice with basic learning skills at each level of education, and they need exercises for reaching higher levels of skills. Student's skills should be improving throughout all the educational levels, since higher education is a goal for most students.

High school students need practice with reading and writing skills that are required for college level study. Students at this level need practice with many forms of note writing to apply the advanced levels of analysis and thinking with study material. They need practice with good quality writing, especially essays and research papers, with an emphasis on higher levels of the thinking and writing skills that are essential for college study. Effective lesson planning should cover these skills.

College students need practice with higher level learning skills that are essential for advanced study programs, for professional careers and for continued learning on their own. Students also need practice with learning skills for each subject matter, and they require practice with suitable practical skills. Students at the college level need assignments that focus on advanced levels of reading, writing and thinking, so they are developing sufficient skills to prepare for advanced levels of functioning.

Students should continue gaining higher level thinking skills throughout all of their educational levels. Six levels of thinking skills have been identified, and they are listed below in order of simple skills to those of greater complexity:

**knowledge, comprehension, analysis
synthesis, evaluation, application**

These thinking levels form the basis for designing study activities that help students advance toward higher levels of analysis and thinking with study material. Discussion is essential to promote better thinking, but it's inadequate without suitable written work for analysis. The higher levels of thinking are best practiced with writing study notes for analysis and thinking, writing essays and research papers along with discussion of the material.

High schools and colleges can provide resource centers for study skills, writing, researching, test preparation, and for career planning and also for teaching. Resource centers can collect and organize information for students and teachers so they can improve their functioning to meet higher level educational goals. High schools can provide classes for motivated students to gain better study and test preparation skills, so students can have the opportunity to optimize their learning and reach greater levels of educational achievement and functioning.

Classroom Activities for Learning
Teachers should assign good quality written work that shows if the students understand study material and remember the key points. Generally, writing a list or outline of key points helps students understand the material better. Then review of study notes can promote greater understanding and thinking.

The best written work for learning is note writing for analysis to increase understanding. Students should be writing suitable notes to analyze various kinds of reading material, with practice writing outlines, summaries and other patterns of notes that increase the ability to process material for thinking and memory. Students who are slower learners or unmotivated for learning require shorter study sessions with more variety to maintain interest. Also these students should have more activities led by the teacher since they need more guidance to develop skills.

Promote the students' reading, writing and thinking skills by assigning appropriate written work for reading assignments and the level of education. Adapt written assignments to promote effective learning in terms of both knowledge and study skills. Students should be expected to complete enough written work to demonstrate their learning of the subject matter, and they should be graded on the quality of their written work.

Since very few tests are available for evaluation, it's wise to base the students' grades on suitable written work. Assign note writing for analysis of their reading material, also to improve learning from verbal and TV presentations. Written notes provide evidence that students' can organize topics in study material, while their written essays show the quality of their thinking.

You might grade writing projects in simple categories such as good, average and poor, even adding a category for excellent. You can grade on the curve by grouping the papers into groups and labeling them as good, average or poor. Also, numbered items might be graded simply in terms of quarters or else by one third of the items to create simple categories for grading.

Although the performance quality will vary, you may find that similar kinds of classroom activities work equally well among the different levels of education.

Examples of Written Work for Elementary Levels

List the key points and topics from your reading assignment

Write outline notes about your assigned reading content

Write various note patterns for different material and goals

Students write study questions to quiz each other in class

List story characters, describing the plot and lessons learned

Students write essays in class to summarize study topics

Practice planning and writing various kinds of written papers

Write short research reports and present verbal summaries

Examples of Elementary Classroom Activities

Students reading in class at least one third of the time

Occasionally students read aloud from various materials

Teacher occasionally reads aloud various materials in class

Students listen to teacher's explanation of study material

Class discussion of study material and written papers

Writing study notes, essays, research and book reports

Written tests of achievement in various subject matter

Students prepare displays of various classroom projects

Teacher led quiz games for review and extra learning

Home Study and Testing

Too many students have poor quality reading and writing skills when they have finished their high school and college education. They haven't gained the level of skills that we expect from what we call "higher education". Employers are using tests to check potential employees for reasonable reading and writing skills. Students also have too much difficulty with achievement testing that's required to graduate from high school and enter college. When your school fails to provide adequate practice with the basic learning skills and preparation for testing requirements, plan a home study program to overcome these deficiencies.

The definition of a good education consists of the functioning requirements we expect for a reasonably well educated person. You can begin with evaluating the knowledge content provided by your school curriculum. Equally important, education should promote higher levels of learning skills, such as reading, writing, speaking, and thinking, Education also should promote research skills for continued learning on your own. Furthermore, students should be prepared to pass the achievement tests required for high school graduation and to enter college.

Problems in Education

* Inadequate strategies for developing higher levels of learning skills with reading, writing and thinking

* Lack of home study resources to review the subject matter required for achievement testing

One problem for students is inadequate learning strategies that fail to promote excellent reading, writing and thinking skills. Students can develop adequate levels of these important skills with practice at home using good learning strategies. Students need practice analyzing reading material by writing study notes. They need practice using good writing strategies for various kinds of written papers. They need to practice problem solving with activities such as the analysis of their study material and writing research reports so they can develop critical thinking skills and communicate their ideas to others.

Achievement testing is another big problem for students, since the school curriculum might not cover some testing topics. Although students might learn subject matter readily, such as math and science, there isn't enough time in school for review. Most students have difficulty remembering enough knowledge and math for required testing. Since high school students usually don't write excellent review notes, they should have materials they can use at home to review subject matter for testing.

Often students have difficulty preparing for school testing that is used to evaluate the quality of their learning. Students should have information about what kinds of testing will be used for their grading, so they can prepare to achieve good grades.

Although strategies for high quality learning can be taught, there are limitations with current forms of testing to show what quality of understanding and learning students have achieved. The following kinds of testing are generally being used, unless teachers can design unique testing for their subject matter.

Typical Testing Options for Grading

Verbal Activity
Recite and Discuss
Explain or Teach Others
Demonstrate Practical Applications

Written Work
Quality of Study Notes
Written Essays about Problems
Longer Written Reports about Problems and Solutions

Typical Testing for Grading
May use Verbal and Written Options above for Grading
Tests with Multiple Choice, Fill in the Blanks and Essay Questions
Longer Written Reports or Explanation of Problems and Solutions

Steps for Planning Home Study

1. **Brief outline of study topics** after locating the material for your knowledge goals

2. **Reading notes** using summaries, outlines and diagrams, and other note patterns for thinking about material

3. **Speaking and discussion** about study material to promote ideas and share your thinking

4. **Review of study notes** for increased thinking and memory

5. **Writing** essays and reports about your reading material

6. **Self-testing** with your review notes about the material

7. **Test preparation** to enter future educational programs and the jobs you prefer

Home Study Begins in Childhood

Formal education can be improved with appropriate home study beginning in childhood. Students learn more in school if parents ask questions about school learning activities and discuss the material. This provides some review and helps students think about the material. Many students need this reinforcement and review of school study content and skills. Sometimes they're not paying enough attention in school, so they fail to learn very well. This problem is easily corrected with occasional review at home, and review also promotes greater interest and success with the activities required for good performance in school.

Use informal tests at home to check if students are gaining suitable knowledge and learning skills for their grade level. Check if students are reading and writing well enough and if they have suitable math skills for their grade level. Students should be learning simple research techniques and doing extra reading at home to explore their interests. They should have adequate opportunities to discuss study topics and research interests with others at home. Encourage them to write summaries and essays about their reading so they can get practice with these skills.

Home study is important to prepare for achievement testing that everyone must deal with throughout their school years. Additional home study promotes better results with the school proficiency testing used to measure student achievement levels.

Study at home provides an opportunity to prepare for numerous forms of achievement testing that students are required to take during the school years. Find suitable test preparation materials that can be used at home to prepare for required testing.

Take children to libraries and bookstores and help them find various kinds of reading materials that promote their interests. Provide a comfortable setting that encourages reading in their spare time. They should have a comfortable reading chair, lamp, bookcase and round table for homework, games and discussion. Encourage them to read and write and discuss ideas. Also read some of these materials with them and summarize the topics. Instead of reading only fiction, also read some non-fiction with them and write summaries for better discussion of the material. Consider establishing a daily reading hour in the evening, or at least occasionally, so they can get in the habit of reading.

Young people might play a variety of games that promote additional skills such as reading game instructions, keeping track of game moves and dealing with the game strategies of others. When learning complex games or computer activities, consider writing lists of instructions to help them learn and remember the rules or steps. Many people require a written summary or list of steps until they can learn to remember all of the instructions required for complex games and computer activities.

Activities at home can provide extra learning experiences that supplement your quality of formal education. Many topics and skills can be covered with activities at home that can't be covered in school because of the time limitations. Explore local opportunities for learning with participation in extra activities and practical skills that help students perform better in school. Students can choose from whatever opportunities are available locally to provide some interesting learning activities.

Family discussion is a good supplementary learning activity, since it promotes improved thinking and communication skills. Discussion promotes important learning skills, such as thinking about material, also organizing and expressing ideas. When students have sufficient opportunities for home discussion, they tend to function better with their school activities.

Discussion is an important activity for improving students' functioning at all ages, since it helps with thinking and solving problems of their concerns. Many older students in high school and college function much better if they have opportunities for discussion about their study material, their problems and their various activities and interests. Students never outgrow the need to develop better thinking and functioning that increases their ability to reach higher levels of learning.

STEPS FOR TEACHING METHODS

Strategies for conducting classroom lessons are described in the teaching textbooks as methods or models of teaching. Steps are listed for each teaching method below that shows the strategy for applying each method. Four categories of teaching models and their specific methods are listed below:

Information Processing Models - Advance Organizer, Concept Attainment, Cognitive Development, Scientific Inquiry Training, Inductive Thinking, Memorization and Synetics
Social Interaction Models - Group Investigation, Individual Learning Styles, Role Playing and Jurisprudential Inquiry
Personal Models - Non-Directive Teaching and Concepts of Self Learning
Behavioral Systems Models - Programmed Instruction, Direct Instruction and Simulations Training

The following summaries of teaching methods are useful for choosing appropriate procedures for teaching or home study. Choose suitable methods for teaching the subject matter and the level of teaching. Consider combining or using parts of various teaching methods to create procedures that meet your specific learning goals. The summaries below are adapted from "Models of Teaching" by Joyce, Weil and Calhoun.

INFORMATION PROCESSING MODELS

ADVANCE ORGANIZER – Introduce these lessons by using the largest concepts for the "advance organizers". Students can understand and remember material better when it's related to large points and concepts that provide anchors for material. Present the large concepts first for this kind of lesson. Then present lower level material and details in an organized form. Large concepts create intellectual maps for learning, since they form anchors that make information more meaningful. When you present higher level ideas first, it provides structure for detailed material so it's more meaningful and also remembered better. The main points are structural concepts for a body of knowledge, and these points should be taught first so they provide mental anchors for better understanding and memory.

Advance organizers are the concepts or else statements of relationships and they should be taught. Advance organizers of material are based on concepts, prepositions, generalizations, principles and the laws of a discipline. These organizers become the structural concepts of each discipline, and they become your information-processing system and intellectual map. Organizers create hierarchically organized sets of ideas like an outline that provides structure for information and ideas. They serve as your mental storehouse for understanding and remembering material.

There are two kinds of organizers:
Expository organizers provide concepts at the highest level of abstraction.
Comparative organizers provide discrimination between new and old material.

STEPS FOR TEACHING WITH ADVANCE ORGANIZERS:
Step One: Present the advance organizers.
Teacher begins by clarifying the aims of the lesson.
Presents the organizer or system of organizers and explains the defining qualities.
Provide context and give some examples or illustrations.
Repeat this process and prompt the learner's awareness of his relevant knowledge and experience.
Step Two: Present the material or learning task.
Present the material, making the organization clear.
Clarify a logical order for studying the material.
Maintain attention and link the material to the organizers.
Step Three: Strengthen the cognitive organization.
General ideas should be presented first, and the generalizations should be followed by organized detailed material.
Integrate organizers with the students' concepts.
Clarify the material and promote critical thinking.
Test new ideas with application and provide practice with skills.

Students' cognitive organization is strengthened by clarifying and by promoting their critical thinking about subject matter. Promote reception to learning by using principles of integrative reconciliation, which means that new ideas should be related to the students' older ideas.

Active learning is promoted by:
1) Students describe how the new material relates to their organizers
2) Students provide more examples of the concept
3) Students verbalize essence of the material
4) Students examine material from alternative views

Your most effective organizers consist of using the concepts, propositions and illustrations that are familiar to the students. This creates intellectual scaffolding for students who are learning more efficiently with organized content as the teacher presents detailed supporting material. Also it's important to continually relate new material to the organizers, and to help students differentiate new material from previous material, so they can integrate new material with the older material they have already learned. With this teaching method, advance organizers are the primary means of strengthening the students' understanding and increasing their memory.

CONCEPT ATTAINMENT – This method teaches students to figure out the higher level concepts or categories for organizing lower level material. This provides practice with the process of forming higher level concepts. Students are given sets of data or samples of information, and they must figure out higher level concepts for their examples. Basically this process consists of grouping and categorizing information and applying inductive reasoning about the qualities of higher level categories.

STEPS FOR TEACHING CONCEPT ATTAINMENT:
Step One: Presenting data and identifying a concept.
Teacher presents the units of data as labeled examples.
Students compare qualities of positive and negative examples.
Students generate and test their own hypotheses.
Students state definition of their concept, and state the rules or definitions in terms of essential qualities.

Step Two: Testing attainment of the concept.
Teacher presents sets of unlabeled data in pairs of positive and negative examples, and the students compare them to find the qualities for concept formation.
Students identify more unlabeled examples.
The teacher confirms the hypotheses, names the concept and restates the definitions.
Students generate their own data examples, and confirm their hypothesis or revise their concepts.

Step Three: Analysis of the thinking strategies.
Students share their thinking strategies and hypotheses.
Students discuss the attributes and the role of hypotheses.
Students analyze their strategies and discuss the type and number of their hypotheses.

"Concept attainment is gained by listing the attributes that are useful to distinguish examples of the concept from non-examples of the concept."

"Concept formation is having students decide the basis or attributes they are using for categories and then name the categories."

This procedure is useful for teaching complex social concepts such as democracy, capitalism, and also due process. Students should compare and contrast their examples to find descriptions for larger categories and to identify characteristics of a category. Students are practicing logical thinking, awareness of alternative explanations and tolerance of ambiguity for many different ideas produced by the other students.

COGNITIVE DEVELOPMENT – This focus is planning for suitable material for the level of intellectual development and maturity of students. The stages of human development are shown by the different kinds of intellectual structures or the concepts found in each stage. Learning is defined as the process of assimilating new material into concepts that are controlled by physical maturation. There are several leading theorists for this method, and they are using slightly different approaches to designing instruction for these concepts about teaching.

The teacher's role is assessing students' thinking, organizing the learning environment and initiating group activities, such as study, games and discussion. Teachers must plan in terms of the students' level of maturity and organize instruction so students can initiate activity and discover the logical connections between their objects and events. The students' role is to be active, self-discovering and also to practice inductive thinking.

STEPS FOR PROMOTING COGNITIVE DEVELOPMENT:
Step One: The teacher presents a suitable task for students' learning needs and then guides the inquiry.
Step Two: The teacher sets up confrontations matched to the students' stage of development so the students must adapt.
Step Three: The teacher provides an open and free social environment, plus a rich physical environment for the student to explore his questions and search for knowledge.
Step Four: The teacher may initiate and guide the inquiry, or it can be student-guided at the higher levels.

<u>Three modes of instruction built around the model of Piaget:</u>
First mode: develop learning situations that pull the students towards more complex thinking.
Second mode: present the students with rules requiring more complex ways of thinking in a language-oriented approach.
Third mode: demonstrating the desired performance clearly for the students.

<u>Three kinds of knowledge:</u>
Physical Knowledge is learning about the nature of matter.
Social Knowledge is learning from feedback of other people.
Logical Knowledge is learning through thinking processes of reflection and abstraction.

<u>Three stages of moral development in cognitive development:</u>
Preconventional Level: Simple concepts of right and wrong
Conventional Level: Conditioned by social conventions
Principled Level: Based upon laws and the Golden Rule

<u>Three "principles of learning" for cognitive development:</u>
1) Teaching is creating an environment for students' cognitive structures to emerge and grow.
2) Learning experiences should be different for each of the three kinds of knowledge.
3) Logical and social knowledge is best learned from the other children.

    SCIENTIFIC INQUIRY TRAINING – This provides practice the steps used by scientific researchers, so this is teaching the method of scientific inquiry. Also it teaches group teamwork and the methods for organizing data. This method helps students to learn procedures for scientific investigation, so they can conduct verbal or physical experiments to test ideas scientifically in terms of their cause and effect relationships. However this method also depends upon students having reasonable access to sufficient material for researching their interests.
    The teacher may help students identify their own hypotheses, collect and interpret their data, and then develop their own concepts or conclusions. With this method, students should be learning to recognize the tentative and emergent nature of their knowledge, as well as that of scientific collections of knowledge they are studying.

STEPS FOR TEACHING WITH SCIENTIFIC INQUIRY:
Step One: Identifying a problem to investigate. Present the problem, present the discrepancies and explain procedures for an inquiry,.
Step Two: Data gathering and verification. Gather data and structure the problem. Students verify the nature of objects and conditions, and verify the occurrence of a problem situation.
Step Three: Data gathering, experimentation. The students isolate variables and hypothesize about relationships in the data, and identify any problems for investigation.
Step Four: Organizing, formulating likely explanations or rules. Find ways to deal with any problems in the investigation. Formulate rules and explanations.
Step Five: Analysis of the inquiry process. Summarize and analyze the students' inquiry process to develop more effective procedures.

Steps for scientific inquiry in biological science:
1) Present an area of investigation to students, and include the methods they should use for inquiry
2) Students structure the problem and find difficulties with the investigation
3) Students identify any problems for their investigation
4) Students think about ways to clear up difficulties in their investigation

INDUCTIVE THINKING – In these lessons, students will practice figuring out the basis for creating higher level categories or large concepts. Begin these lessons by presenting detailed material so students might figure out the generalizations and larger concepts for the material. Students learn about concept formation by classifying data and forming categories. Students learn these skills from differentiating, abstracting, determining cause and effect and from finding implications. These activities are teaching students about creating and organizing data sets for concept formation, which is the basis for higher level thinking skills such as analysis and synthesis.

Three assumptions for teaching thinking.
1) Thinking can be taught as an orderly sequence.
2) Thinking is an active transaction of students and data.
3) Students' thought processes evolve by a process that is lawful and orderly.

First, present the students with sets of data about a topic. Then they organize their data sets into conceptual patterns and generalize about relationships they discover, making inferences that hypothesize, predict and explain the phenomena. Students should use study methods such as questioning and discussion to learn about interpreting, inferring and generalizing. Students should practice applying their principles to explain new material. They can do this by using the processes such as predicting, explaining and verifying their new knowledge.

STEPS FOR INDUCTIVE THINKING LESSONS:

Phase One - Concept formation   A collection of data is provided by the teacher, or else the students are instructed to collect and categorize information.

Step One: Students begin these lessons by counting and listing the relevant data for a problem.

Step Two: Student activity is listing, grouping, labeling and categorizing. Their goals are differentiation, identifying common properties and determining the hierarchical order of items. Their questions consist of what you see and how you group the items.

Step Three: The students should arrange data into categories that have common qualities and label their categories.

Phase Two - Interpretation of the data Students develop an understanding about relationships in their data and among the categories or concepts.

Step Four: Students identify the critical relationships

Step Five: Students explore those relationships

Step Six: Students make inferences. The student thinking is relating, differentiating, extrapolating and finding implications. Their questions are what was noticed, why this happened, what it means and what conclusions may be drawn. Their application of principles requires predicting consequences, explaining the unfamiliar phenomena and then hypothesizing. Students should explain or support their predictions and hypotheses, and finally try to verify their predictions.

Phase Three - Application of principles

Step Seven: This activity consists of predicting consequences by explaining, verifying, supporting and hypothesizing.

Step Eight: Explaining or supporting the predictions and the hypotheses. Thinking to analyze the nature of the problem, find relevant data, predict the causes and use logical principles.

Step Nine: Verifying the prediction. Questions are what and why would this happen, and what would make this be true.

MEMORIZATION – The focus of this method is providing practice with using better quality strategies for memorizing material. To promote better memory from learning, first we must pay attention to remember something. Additionally, we need to pay attention in a form that we are rehearsing for later recall. When we rehearse information, we can develop retrieval cues for the material. You can use devices like the link-word method that are more effective than natural memory methods. The best methods for improving upon memory are listed below.

The ability to remember a reasonable amount of material from learning is fundamental for intellectual effectiveness. For practical applications, the memory techniques that work best are: organizing the information or putting it into a meaningful order, linking information to form associations or relationships, linking to words, linking to associated information and linking to visuals and sounds. Finally some practice or rehearsal is important to enhance your memory process and this is usually called "review".

STEPS FOR TEACHING WITH THE MEMORY MODEL:
Step One: Attention to the material using techniques like underlining, listing and reflecting
Step Two: Developing connections by using the key words, substitute words and link-word system techniques
Step Three: Expanding sensory images with association, exaggeration and revising the images
Step Four: Practicing recall of the study material until it's completely learned

Concepts for developing memory
Awareness or concentrating on the material
Association or making connections for learning
Link system of connecting material or forming relationships
Ridiculous association that's vivid
Substitute word system to make idea memorable or graphic
Key word that represents a larger group of material

Memorization Strategies

1) Organizing the information to be learned
2) Ordering the information to be learned
3) Linking information to familiar material or sounds
4) Linking information to visual representations
5) Linking information to associated information
6) Making information vivid with devices like dramatization
7) Rehearsing and reviewing and reciting

SYNETICS – These lessons apply procedures for creativity to occur, so this method trains students for increased creativity. Creative steps help students to see familiar things in unfamiliar ways and vice versa, so that students are developing new perspectives and finding new solutions to their problems. Creativity is important in our everyday activities, and creativity can be taught by using suitable procedures. Creative invention is a similar activity for solving all kinds of problems, and these procedures are the same for groups and individuals.

This method is easily combined with other teaching methods, and it's useful for all age levels. The group activity is used to generate energy. The teacher stimulates group discussion that promotes creativity. Also the teacher guards against premature analysis and closure. This process enlarges your understanding and improves your creative capacity. This method is helpful for students who are afraid to participate because they are afraid of being wrong, since this encourages their creative responses.

The uses for synetics lessons: creative writing, problem solving, exploring social problems, creating a design or a product and broadening your perspective about a concept

STEPS FOR THE SYNETICS METHOD OF TEACHING:
Step One: The original product Find a problem, product or topic to explore
Step Two: Direct and personal analogies Students make comparisons using analogies
Step Three: Compressed conflicts and oxymoronic analogies Define conflicts and continue eliciting material from students until their examples are both logical and illogical
Step Four: Generating new products Use creative material with the original problem to redefine the problem and to generate alternate solutions

Three kinds of metaphors used for these thinking activities:
Direct Analogy. A simple comparison of two objects or use concepts to find a new perspective
Personal Analogy. Students should identify with the idea or the object to feel involved
Compressed Conflict. Express opposites or contradictions to increase learner's mental flexibility

Steps for creating something new:

One: Description of the present condition. Formulate a topic or problem to explore, record the students current thoughts, and have the students describe the current condition.

Two: Direct analogy. Use direct analogy exercises or make comparisons, and select one to explore further.

Three: Personal analogy. Make personal analogies by placing yourself in the position of the items examined. Ask the students to describe it and imagine they are the analogy.

Four: Compressed conflict. Create compressed conflicts from the material generated in the previous step and choose one.

Five: Direct analogy. Students select another direct analogy based upon the compressed conflict, and they generate new products and solutions to problems from ideas that were generated previously.

Six: Reexamination of the original task. Students reexamine their original topic, use their last analogy, and review their entire experience.

Steps for making the strange familiar:

One: Substantive input. Teacher provides the information for a new topic.

Two: Direct analogy. Teacher suggests the analogy and asks students to describe an analogy.

Three: Personal analogy. Encourage students to "become" the direct analogy.

Four: Comparing analogies. The students explain similarities between the new material and their direct analogy.

Five: Explaining differences. Students explain where the analogy doesn't fit.

Six: Exploration. Students explore the original topic again, within its own terms.

Seven: Generating analogy. The students provide their own direct analogy to explore the similarities and differences.

Assumptions about the nature of creativity:
1) We can increase creativity with a conscious process
2) The emotional component is far more important than the rational component
3) The emotional and irrational elements must be understood to increase creativity

SOCIAL INTERACTION MODELS

GROUP INVESTIGATION – Learning within a social group is the focus of this method. Organize students into groups to work on solving problems together, so they can be problem-solvers learning about scientific inquiry and democratic procedures. These lessons should begin with a problem or inquiry for the group to investigate. The group discusses their reactions to the problem. Then students organize study by writing a problem definition and by distributing individual roles and assignments. They proceed with both group and independent study. Finally they analyze their progress, evaluate their processes and recycle the activity to search for solutions or knowledge.

The teacher encourages the group processes by functioning as a coach and counselor and by intervening to channel group energy into productive learning. The teacher supervises the group activities so that inquiry continues until the students' knowledge comes from their group learning experiences.

STEPS FOR TEACHING WITH GROUP INVESTIGATION
Step One: Encounter a puzzling situation. Students are puzzled or presented with a problem to solve
Step Two: Explore reactions to the situation. Students explore their reactions to the problem or situation
Step Three: Formulate study task and organize study. Students formulate and organize their study tasks
Step Four: Independent and group study. Students proceed with independent and group study
Step Five: Analyze progress and process. Students analyze their progress and their process
Step Six: Recycle activity. Students repeat this process and their activity to find solutions

Two concepts are basic in this teaching model:
Inquiry is the starting point for learning, and it consists of finding a problem
Knowledge is the result of the problem solving activity

Students begin a lesson by reacting to problems and defining them, so they can discover differences of thinking, attitudes and styles of perception. They clarify the problem to be studied, and then analyze what roles are required for the group to work on the problem. They organize themselves into these roles, and then analyze, evaluate and report their results. Use small teachable groups for these kinds of lessons, since these lessons require teamwork like the workplace for solving their problems. This process requires learning to work within groups to discover one's own knowledge needs and style of learning. This procedure requires good media resources or a research library for the students to find information about problems. For these lessons, it's important to write the problem definition, the procedures used and data collected, and then the summary or conclusions.

INDIVIDUAL LEARNING STYLES – This method focuses on the learner's mental complexity of information processing so the learning environment can be matched to the learner's stage of maturity or complexity. These lessons begin with the teacher estimating the students' mental maturity, and then teaching to help students reach higher levels of cognitive complexity.

The teacher should plan the learning environment to promote greater learning complexity, so that students are learning at optimal rates while increasing in the complexity of their thinking skills. The teacher should provide greater learning structure for lower level students. As students increase in mental complexity, they should be learning to direct more of their own activities with the group investigation approach to learning.

Four levels of cognitive complexity are defined:
Stage One: Low complexity. Characterized by extremely fixed patterns of response, and also by low complexity of simple, categorical black and white thinking.
Stage Two: Moderate complexity. Active resistance to authority, and still showing simple responses to environment. Moderate cognitive complexity and able to generate alternative organizations, thus moving away from their absolute and simple views.
Stage Three: Moderately high complexity. Beginning to see the viewpoints of others and to balance alternatives. Moderately high complexity consists of combining and balancing alternative viewpoints and the ways of interpreting things.
Stage Four: High complexity. Can maintain balanced perspective about work orientation and interpersonal relations. High complexity includes more potential for adapting to change and new information.

For learners of low complexity, plan for a highly structured environment and clearly define the tasks. For learners of higher complexity, arrange for an interdependent and emerging environment so students are growing in the ability to direct their own activities. By matching students to an appropriate learning environment for their level of maturity, they can develop more flexibility and complexity in their personalities. Students are continually growing in terms of their self-awareness and the ability to manage their own educational activities.

STEPS FOR BASIC TASKS IN THIS TEACHING MODEL:
Step One: the teacher should differentiate the students' mental complexity or development levels.
Step Two: the teacher matches the learning environment to the complexity of students.
Step Three: the environment and training is planned to increase the mental complexity of students.

ROLE PLAYING –Solving the problems of social interaction is the focus of this method. A problem is identified, acted out and then discussed to share experiences. The students can learn to recognize roles they play and why they're playing these roles. Students can learn about problems in human relationships by exploring their feelings, values and problem solving strategies together. They can develop problem solving skills, explore their feelings and gain insight into their attitudes, values and outlook. These activities also help students learn about solving problems together as a group, and they improve their skills for negotiating and understanding the roles of others.

Various kinds of problems can be studied with role-playing, such as typical inter-group relations and interpersonal conflicts, individual dilemmas and historical or contemporary problems. The values to emphasize in role-playing are subject matter exploration, the exploration of feelings, exploration of attitudes, values and perceptions and the development of problem-solving skills and attitudes. By role playing, students learn to explore subject matter in different ways.

Teachers use the following five principles of reaction:
1) Accept students' responses, suggestions, opinions and feelings without value statements
2) Respond in a manner that helps students to explore various sides of issues
3) Reflect, paraphrase and summarize the student responses to increase their awareness
4) Emphasize the different ways that roles can be played with different consequences
5) Emphasize alternate ways to solve a problem and that no one way is correct

STEPS FOR ROLE-PLAYING LESSONS:
Step One: Warm up the group by identifying a problem and making the problem explicit. Interpret the problem story. Explore the issues and explain the role-playing.
Step Two: Select participants or the role players and analyze the roles.
Step Three: Set the stage and create the first line of action. Restate the roles and problems and set a course or get inside the problem situation.
Step Four: Prepare the observers. Decide what to look for and assign the observation tasks.
Step Five: The enactment. Begin and maintain role-playing to an ending point.
Step Six: Discuss and evaluate the role-playing. Review action and discuss the focus, plan a reenactment, and then analyze to share the experiences.
Step Seven: Reenact the revised roles, and suggest the next steps or the alternative behaviors.
Step Eight: Discuss and evaluate as in step six.
Step Nine: Share experiences and generalize by relating the problems to real experiences and by exploring the general principles of behavior.

Areas of learning focus for role playing
Exploring and acting out feelings
Clarifying attitudes, values and perceptions
Identifying and solving problems, experiencing consequences
Exploring subject matter, dilemmas and decisions

JURISPRUDENTIAL INQUIRY –This method consists of debating public policy issues, and it works better with older students such as junior high school and higher levels. Identify a social problem so the class can research and discuss the issue. This method teaches analysis of public issues and respect for differences of the other students' opinions and values. Students take a position and the others challenge that position with their questions. Socratic dialogue is used to argue the positions. The goal is creating discussion that illustrates how social policy develops, while showing respect for students' different views.

In this method, students learn by arguing the pros and cons of each viewpoint. They can choose a view or position, defend that view, and then they can revise their positions through argumentation. This method provides practice with analyzing public issues while clarifying the students' values. To work well, the students should have some knowledge about the broader historical, political, economic and sociological background of problems. Students must understand the framework of legal-ethical values, also Socratic dialogue and public policy issues.

Student arguments try to clarify three kinds of problems:
Problems of definition
Problems of value
Problems of factual information

STEPS FOR TEACHING WITH JURISPRUDENTIAL INQUIRY:
Step One: Orientation to the case. Open up the issues, introduce the materials and review the facts.
Step Two: Identify the issues. Synthesize facts into public policy issues, and select one for discussion. Identify values and value conflicts. Recognize the underlying questions of facts and definition. Examine the options and values and conflicts.
Step Three: Taking positions. Express a position or an opinion, and state the basis for your position in terms of social values or consequences.
Step Four: Exploring the stance and the patterns of argumentation. Establish points at which a value is violated. Prove the desirable or undesirable consequences of your position. Clarify the value conflict with analogies. Set priorities. Assert the priority of one value over another, and demonstrate the lack of violation of a second value.
Step Five: Refining and qualifying the positions. State the positions and the reasons underlying your positions, and examine numerous similar situations. Qualify your position, and modify positions and make recommendations according to the previous discussion.
Step Six: Testing factual assumptions behind the qualified positions. Try to identify the factual assumptions and determine if they are relevant. Try to predict consequences and examine their factual validity.

Students may use four patterns of argumentation:
1) Students identify point at which a value is violated
2) Students clarify value conflict through analogies
3) Students try to prove good or bad consequences of their positions
4) Students set priorities of values, asserting the priority of one value and showing lack of violation of the second value

PERSONAL MODELS

NON-DIRECTIVE TEACHING – This teaching method is based on the client-centered psychology theory of Carl Rogers. This method defines learning as a process of self reorganization as the personality is being constructed. A learner can be trusted to desire learning and to make use of his resources for learning. Also a learner is competent to direct himself. We cannot teach others, but we can only facilitate learning and a learner learns what he perceives as enhancing to himself. Students define the problems and purposes they have, and then they build a course of study that meets their interests and goals. The teacher's role is organizing resources and students choose the topics.

STEPS FOR NON-DIRECTIVE TEACHING EPISODES:
Step One: Defining the helping situation. The teacher encourages free expression of feelings, so that students are encouraged to define problems, and the teacher accepts and clarifies the feelings.
Step Two: Exploring the problem. Students are encouraged to discuss and define problems and then express their negative and positive opinions. The teacher accepts and clarifies the feelings and possible decisions.
Step Three: Developing insight. Student discusses problems and the teacher is supportive. The student gains insight and sees new relationships.
Step Four: Planning and decision-making. The students proceed with planning and decision making about their problems and report their actions. The teacher clarifies possible decisions that students are considering.
Step Five: Integration. The students gain more insight and develop more positive actions, and the teacher is supportive. The students report their actions and plan more integrated and positive actions.

Teacher's responses in discussion
Non-Directive Responses to Feelings: Simple acceptance, Reflect feelings, Paraphrase content.

Lead-taking Non-Directive Responses: Structuring, directive questioning, and encouraging students to choose and develop topics, Use non-directive leads and open questions, Minimal encouragement to talk should be provided for students.

The students decide what's important to learn and they select methods for learning. The teacher should be nonjudgmental, and a facilitator of the students' self-directed learning. This model deals with the emotional element of students' behavior and thinking. It clarifies the students' present feelings, their distorted perceptions and alternative solutions they have not explored because of their emotional reactions to them.

The teacher leads the study by "structuring the situation", by questioning, by encouraging discussion, and by getting students to choose and develop their topics. These activities are not prescribed but are determined by learners as they interact with the teacher and the other students. The teacher's response to expressed feelings from the students can be simple acceptance, reflection of feelings or else simply paraphrasing content.

The teacher's role is non-directive, so the students are taking responsibility for initiating and maintaining learning within their group interaction. This non-directive approach focuses on the emotional reactions of students rather than on content, and it lets students direct the flow of their thoughts and feelings.

CONCEPTS OF SELF LEARNING– The learning differences among students are caused by how much they tend to interact with their environment productively for learning. Students learn according to their states of maturity and self-concepts that affect how much they interact with others and their environment. It's been shown that learners will vary in the amount of interest and interaction for learning they show with their environment.

People who are more successful have shown higher levels of learning activity both personally and professionally. They draw more attention from their environment and they bring more possibilities into their reach. They have learned to survey their environment and use it successfully for progress with learning. Strong self-concepts are connected with behavior that's more productive for "self-actualizing" or learning.

Conceptual systems theory describes people in terms of the structure of concepts they use to organize information. In lower stages of development, learners use few concepts and hold onto them rigidly. In higher stages, learners have greater ability to tolerate new views, integrate new information, and to modify their structure of concepts. Higher level learners have more complex conceptual structures, and they continually search for more productive ways of organizing information. They are more likely to reach for new experiences and learn to deal with them.

The students' goal is learning how to learn better, and this increases their ability to continue with additional learning. The school environment can influence how students interact and how much they will reach for higher levels of learning.

STEPS FOR APPLYING CONCEPTS OF SELF LEARNING:
Step One: If students are provided with enough opportunity for learning, all students can learn and respond to great variety in their learning environments.

Step Two: The more skills that students are learning, they more they improve their ability to continue learning with greater ranges of skills and strategies.

Step Three: The school creates the social learning environment for good quality learning that's dynamic and productive interaction with the environment.

Students' levels of interest for learning:
1) Reticent students who avoid opportunities for learning
2) Passive students whose activity depends upon the context or the environment
3) Active students who are quite engaged in finding learning opportunities
4) Gourmet students who vigorously seek new opportunities for learning and growth

BEHAVIORAL SYSTEMS MODELS

PROGRAMMED INSTRUCTION or MASTERY LEARNING – This learning program presents small sequences of instruction that are planned to achieve "mastery learning". This learning sequence usually begins with diagnosis or tests. Then suitable learning materials are organized and the form of instructional strategy is selected. The student's ability is defined in terms of the amount of time needed for learning, and also by the style of instruction that works best for the student.

These learning activities are divided into small units, and each unit is defined by goals for the student. Mastery is defined in terms of goals that represent the purpose of the units. The results from diagnostic tests can be used to design additional instruction until the student overcomes his learning deficiencies. This procedure provides enough time for each student to learn at his own pace and in terms of his own ability for learning.

"Individually Prescribed Instruction", also called IPI's, is the method of teaching that designs unique programmed learning sequences for students with learning disabilities or with unusual learning styles. These students will need more time or else specifically designed sequences to practice their academic skills than is provided in a regular classroom. The individualized instruction should promote self-initiation and self-direction in learning. It enables students to work at their own rates to reach the appropriate levels of mastery for their goals.

Three features are required for good programmed instruction. First, it must be an ordered sequence of items or questions that requires a response from the learner. Second, the student must respond in some form. Third, the student must see immediately if his responses to problems are correct or not. Generally these procedures are useful to design self-teaching programs for students in the form of workbooks, learning games or computer learning programs.

STEPS TO PLAN INDIVIDUALLY PRESCRIBED INSTRUCTION:
Step One: Systems analysis is used to develop a modular curriculum that enables students to work at their own rate of mastery, develop problem solving, self-evaluation and improved motivation for learning
Step Two: Analyze a set of organized behavioral objectives to develop degree of mastery
Step Three: Develop self-initiation and self-direction for the learning process
Step Four: Foster the development of problem solving through the instructional processes
Step Five: Encourage self-evaluation and motivation for greater personal learning

PROGRAMMED INSTRUCTION APPLIES THESE STEPS:
First: Mastery of a subject is defined in terms of the major objectives and purposes of study
Second: Learning material is divided into small units in terms of the objectives
Third: Learning materials are identified and the instructional strategy is selected
Fourth: Each unit of learning is followed by diagnostic tests that measure progress and may reinforce learning
Fifth: Data or information from diagnostic tests is used to provide the supplementary education that helps each student overcome specific learning problems

DIRECT INSTRUCTION –This common teaching method contains the following five steps: orientation, presentation, structured practice, guided practice and independent practice. This kind of instruction might begin with a diagnostic test of the students' knowledge or skills so you can be certain that the instruction is appropriate for the students. This basic method of teaching consists of the teacher explaining a new skill or concept to the students, and then students' test their understanding by practicing the new skill while the teacher monitors their activity. Direct instruction has been found to work better for some kinds of subject matter and for slower learners.

STEPS FOR TEACHING WITH DIRECT INSTRUCTION:
Step One: Orientation or presenting the framework for the lesson. Clarify the goals, tasks and the student accountability. The teacher reviews previous learning, presents the objective and level of performance required. Then the teacher describes the content and procedures of the lesson.

Step Two: Presentation of the lesson with teacher explaining the new material and providing examples or demonstrations. Identify any steps required, present material in various ways such as orally in addition to visually, and check for adequate understanding and recall.

Step Three: Structured practice means the teacher leads students through examples for practice that shows students how to do the work. The teacher provides feedback.

Step Four: Guided practice is the next stage that provides an opportunity for students to practice on their own with the teacher monitoring and checking their work.

Step Five: Independent practice until students have reached a high level of accuracy, and the practice reinforces learning to achieve better memory of the material.

The practice activities are important for direct instruction. Students need experience with several levels of practice until they can perform a skill independently and without error. After the guided group practice, students should continue practicing by themselves until they can perform the tasks correctly. Short and more frequent practice sessions were found to be more effective than longer sessions that are less frequent. Also distributed practice that's spread over more time is better, and later the practice sessions can be spaced more widely without having students forget their new skills.

Principles for the practice activities of direct instruction:

One: Shape learning by the levels of practice. Students practice with different levels of teacher assistance until independence is achieved. First, the teacher leads the group through each step of the problem. Next, students' practice by themselves while the teacher monitors the activity. Finally after accuracy is achieved, the students can perform independent practice.

Two: The practice sessions should not be very long, and shorter intense sessions work better.

Three: Monitor beginning performance to prevent students from learning the wrong performance.

Four: Reach a high level of accuracy before going to the next level with practice activities.

Five: Use distributed practice and multiple sessions spread out over time since this reinforces material.

Six: The optimal time between practice sessions should be closer together when the student is beginning to learn, and later they can be spaced out more.

SIMULATIONS TRAINING – This method applies principles of cybernetic psychology to training procedures, and it uses a mechanical game or simulator to train students in complex skills. Computer software is used for most simulations, and this creates processes that look like computer gaming. These procedures are important when learning to operate complex machinery. The advantage of using simulators is that the tasks are less complex than the real world, so that training can be staged.

The learner performs as a self-regulating feedback system, since he can adjust his performance in terms of the results he's getting. So the learner is redirecting or correcting his action as necessary. The simulators enable students to learn from their self-generated feedback so they are largely self-instructing. Learning activity is controlled by the student, while the teacher's role consists of explaining, coaching, refereeing and discussion.

The teacher prepares the learning environment by selecting materials and by directing the specific simulation activities. The class environment should be relaxed and cooperative, and the teacher's role is that of referee and coach, by using explanation and discussion. The teacher helps students cope with problems as they arise during their learning and practice activities. The teacher takes care of the organization of materials, explaining the game, setting the rules, giving advice and then monitoring discussion after the learning activity.

STEPS FOR SIMULATIONS TRAINING:

Step One: Orientation. Instruction begins with the teacher presenting the topic and concepts, explaining the simulator and gaming, and then presenting an overview of the simulation.

Step Two: Participant training. The teacher sets up the rules and procedures, the scoring and the scenario. The roles are assigned and students try a small practice session.

Step Three: Simulation operations. The game activity is conducted. Students obtain feedback and evaluation, they clarify their problems and continue the simulation game.

Step Four: Participant debriefing. Summarize the process and problems by examining these events with understanding. Summarize the problems and understanding. Analyze processes by comparing simulation to the real world, and by relating it to the course content. Students should appraise and redesign their simulation activity as they might consider necessary. Students continue to apply and practice these processes until adequate levels of proficiency are reached for the skills they are learning.

These methods of teaching can be simply applied by using the steps listed with each method. Your job is to evaluate which method will be effective for your students' learning abilities, your specific study material and your learning goals for the class. Using a variety of methods creates more interest in learning for the students while it provides practice with additional learning skills and styles of learning. Also you can combine elements from the various methods to create new learning experiences.

Quick Steps for Planning Learning/Teaching

Begin with school curriculum goals and materials available

Outline study topics briefly and distribute in time schedule

Choose the reading assignments first and schedule them

Choose written work and testing that increases learning

Choose suitable activities for practice with learning skills

Consider what teaching methods to use with the material

Plan for suitable homework and the standards for grading

Write summary planning in planning book or as a syllabus

Write daily planning to implement your summary planning

Outline planning for classroom activities with flexible time

5 EDUCATION AND WORK

Educational Planning Steps

USE ORIENTATION INFORMATION and summaries for an understanding of the options

SORT JOB GROUPS with the three common educational levels for work

CONSIDER EDUCATION GOALS or school performance for career choice

SURVEY DECISION METHODS and important issues to consider for career choice

REVIEW THE OPTIONS for thinking about educational decisions

STEPS FOR ORIENTATION

Many students have great difficulty choosing educational goals in high school and college, because they lack knowledge about how education relates to future work options. Educational decisions in higher education depend on knowledge about what education is required for specific jobs. Many careers require specific levels of education and testing, so your planning might begin during high school and continue long term as you consider higher levels of education. When you learn about the work options during your school years, you can plan for your educational goals.

Planning for your future begins with orientation information about education and work. Begin with the largest categories of options first. If you're only using detailed information, you won't reach comprehensive understanding about all of the options. It's important to start with an introduction to the largest categories of work options. Then you only need to sort detailed information about those options you want to explore more fully.

Understanding your options requires orientation information. Begin by exploring all the large job categories in Appendix B, showing how work relates to most common educational levels. The section about education and testing explains how school performance and test scores relate to your educational options so you can plan these goals. Use job outlook information to help you identify jobs with good employment opportunities and avoid jobs lacking in opportunities. Then you might want to compare earnings information about jobs, explore career decision-making strategies and get an introduction to job hunting. The categories of information below are useful for planning future goals.

Information to Plan Education and Work

Education and Schools – What educational programs and levels do you prefer, and how do they relate to work options? What information can be found for comparing costs among the educational options, and how does the quality of educational programs and your grades relate to work goals?

Testing – What kinds of testing are required for the options in education and work?

Occupations – What categories and groups of jobs are found in our economy, and how do these jobs relate to the educational options and levels? What long-term planning for promotions can help you choose suitable education and work experience to reach your future goals?

Job Outlook – What jobs have good quality opportunities for employment, and what jobs lack sufficient opportunities or are found in only a few locations?

Income – How can you compare the income and benefits for your work interests and long-term work goals?

Methods of Career Decision – What strategies can help you find your best educational and work options?

Job Hunting and Application – What you need is a resume, cover letter, reference list, and speaking notes for interviews. Consider what job hunting methods to use, and what job search help may be available from your local resources?

For each category of information required for future planning, you need an introduction to good quality orientation resources. Information about education and work might be found in many locations, but you might not find the best resources you need to be well informed. You should be able to find good information resources online when you can't find them in your local library. The best online orientation resources for work and education are listed below. This is followed by summaries of planning strategy and orientation lists in the appendixes.

ORIENTATION INFORMATION FOR PLANNING

Job Information from the Bureau of Labor Statistics

"Standard Occupational Classification Manual"(SOC), lists job groups in 23 categories, was found at: www.bls.gov/soc

"O*NET Dictionary of Occupational Titles" was found at: www.onetonline.org

"O*NET Resource Center-Career Exploration Tools" provides self-directed career exploration at: www.onetcenter.org/tools.html

"Dictionary of Occupational Titles" (DOT) This older version was found at: www.occupationalinfo.org

"Career One Stop" has America's Career Infonet, State Job Banks, and other tools, found at: www.careeronestop.org

"Career Information for Students" shows 13 categories of job interest areas to help with exploring careers

Job Outlook and Earnings Information at: www.bls.gov

(These publications and titles are changing occasionally)

"Occupational Outlook Handbook" has information about 250 jobs and summaries for 116 jobs

"Occupational Outlook Quarterly" has updated information

"Employment by Occupations" shows another viewpoint of the outlook information

"Wages by Area and Occupation" shows the regional trends and differences

"Employment and Earnings" shows the current employment statistics

National Compensation Survey: Occupational Earnings in the United States 2006"

"Employment and Wages" shows current weekly and hourly wages for occupations

Educational Programs and Schools

"A Classification of Instructional Programs" was found at:
http://nces.ed.gov/pubs2002/cip2000

From the College Entrance Examination Board
"College Handbook, Book of College Majors"
"College Costs, Financial Aid and Scholarships Handbook"
"Handbook of All Accredited 2 Year and 4 Year Colleges"

Peterson's Guides to Educational Programs and to Colleges
"Guide to Technical and Vocational Schools"
"Guide to 4 Year Colleges"
"Guide to Financial Aid and Scholarships"

"The World Almanac Book of Facts"
Shows the cost comparison for all USA colleges
Shows the average test scores for the SAT and ACT college
entrance tests in each state

Testing, Career Decision and Job Hunting
Specific resources aren't listed here for these categories, since
many guides are available in libraries and bookstores. If you
can't find the test practice guides you want in bookstores and
libraries, see the web sites of test guide publishers where you
can find guides to cover essentially all variations of testing that
can be expected for your options in education and work.

ORIENTATION TO WORK

Understanding Your Options
The most important information needed for planning educational
goals is an orientation to work options. Individual job titles are
too numerous to sort for good understanding about job options.
You can only understand the options comprehensively by using
an information source about the largest categories and groups of
jobs first. Then you may sort within these categories and groups
for specific titles that you want to explore more fully.

You can understand work options better when job titles are
organized into groups and categories. Organized titles help you
understand the related options in large groups and categories.
Organized job titles help you find all the related jobs you can
work in with each educational program that you might choose.
Comparing groups of related jobs helps you understand these
options better, so you can identify your strongest interests and
choose suitable education to prepare for work goals.

Many small variations of job titles are found in our economy, because employers create these variations for small promotions. Sorting small variations of job titles is more distracting than helpful for career planning. Small variations of job titles don't add meaningful information for planning your educational goals. Also they don't help with collecting meaningful job statistics, and therefore many variations of job titles have been dropped from newer editions of the Dictionary of Occupational Titles.

Very few information resources show all of the largest groups and categories of jobs. Many resources are incomplete except those from the Bureau of Labor Statistics, and it may be difficult to find some of these resources. A random selection might be available in your library reference section, so you need to know how to find good resources online. Use the lists above to find the best online resources for each category of information you want. Many comprehensive information resources about work can be found on the Bureau of Labor Statistics web site.

You can find many arrangements of work groups that might enhance your understanding of the options, but you only need one comprehensive source showing all of the work categories and groups. The most comprehensive orientation resources are collections of job titles by the Bureau of Labor Statistics that are called the Standard Occupational Classification Manual (SOC), and the Dictionary of Occupational Titles (DOT).

The SOC collection of job titles has better quality job titles and organization for some work groups than the older DOT. This provides more clarity about the related jobs. See Appendix B for the largest categories of SOC titles arranged into three common educational levels. This provides an introduction to the largest categories of work, and it shows the corresponding educational levels commonly used to prepare for these work categories.

Older editions of the DOT describe over 20,000 variations of job titles. More recent editions of the DOT have reduced these titles to about 12,000 job titles. The new online dictionary of occupational titles, called the O*NET database, has reduced these to approximately 1,000 job titles. Also the new O*NET collection of job titles includes more general information about each job, such as income and job outlook, that previously was only available in the "Occupational Outlook Handbook".

The new O*NET Dictionary of Occupational Titles only covers about 1,000 job titles organized into groups, but this functions efficiently for sorting the basic work options in our economy. Always begin with the largest job groups and categories to understand all of your options. Then sort lower level job titles of interest. Also sort for any unusual job titles that are not well represented by their group title.

For each job title, the O*NET Dictionary provides basic job information such as: description of the work, the educational requirements, the average annual earnings, the number of people currently employed and the estimated future outlook for employment growth. Libraries usually have a print version that's called the "O*NET Dictionary of Occupational Titles".

See the library reference area for the new O*NET Dictionary of Occupational Titles. This book helps you sort jobs from five different viewpoints. You can sort jobs by categories showing the related job groups in each category. You can sort alphabetically or by education and training programs. Also you can sort jobs by work skills and 14 interest areas. This new O*NET also shows the top 50 jobs in terms of the best paying, the fastest growing and jobs with the most employment openings.

The O*NET web site provides additional ways to sort jobs. You can explore the work requirements for 16 career clusters of job titles. You can explore jobs by education and industry and by "bright outlook". You can sort by 20 job families, by the STEM subject matter and by apprenticeships. Also you may find many related web sites online that can help you explore jobs from different perspectives and with different information. You can enter job codes from other government publications, such as DOT, MOC, CIP and RAIS to see corresponding job titles in the O*NET job groups. (MOC is Military Occupational Classification, RAIS is the Registered Apprenticeship Information System and CIP is the Classification of Instructional Programs).

In older editions of the DOT, you can see numerous job title variations that each job might be called among employers. Also the DOT describes the work duties for each variation of job title. This helps you explore variations of work more fully for your interest areas, but you can expect that employers will continue changing these variations of titles and duties. You can see the SOC, DOT and the O*Net online, also in the reference section of libraries or in the government documents collection.

Explore detailed job information by beginning with resources such as the "O*NET Dictionary of Occupational Titles" and the "Occupational Outlook Manual". These resources cover the larger job groups in our economy, and they provide more detailed information for comparing the common jobs. See the Bureau of Labor Statistics and also US Department of Labor web sites for additional information resources about work. Also check local libraries to explore what career information collections they have available, and check online with various search terms to explore any information resources listed there. Also talk to people who are working in jobs you find interesting, and prepare questions to ask them about your job concerns.

Using Job Outlook Information

If you want good employment opportunities with career choice so it's easy to find work, compare job outlook information for all the jobs you're considering. However if you have strong interests and abilities for work with a weak employment outlook, then you may be able to compete better for the limited work opportunities that are available for your job choice.

The job outlook estimates the how much work opportunity is expected in terms of the current job market size or how many people are currently employed in each work group. Information about outlook is an estimate of the work opportunity you can expect in the near future for each group or category of work.

Job outlook information can be found in the O*NET Dictionary of Occupational Titles and in other publications by the Bureau of Labor Statistics. Outlook information describes the national job market, so it's worth estimating the local employment trends if you only want to work in certain locations.

You can estimate the local job outlook by checking quantities of job ads that you find in newspapers or on career web sites for locations of interest. List your job groups of interest, and sort the quantity of ads in local newspapers and online to estimate the quantity of your local opportunities.

Another source of outlook information is talking to people who keep up with local business news, or else people who have lived in an area long enough to notice the job market and local business trends. Try to explore a variety of resources about your local job outlook. You might check the Chamber of Commerce, job ads and the local employment agencies. Also check online to look for up-to-date resources about job outlook information.

Some outlook information is found in business news stories. For example, news stories might report the development of new technologies, and this indicates jobs might be available soon to work with these new technologies. Focus on information indicating what job titles or groups are currently in greatest demand. Large trends in the labor market also indicate what changes may be expected in manufacturing or the specific job categories. Career planning can be focused more efficiently when you have information about the general job market trends and about specific jobs that you find interesting.

When the economic trends are indicating a weak job market, it's important to choose work with a good employment outlook and to obtain suitable education for work. Then you have more opportunities for employment. However it's always wise to have alternative jobs in mind that can keep you working when the job market becomes weak for your career choice.

Comparing Earnings

Will your income from work provide a good standard of living? Compare wages for your work interests by exploring the wage publications from the Bureau of Labor Statistics. Also you may find helpful information in newspaper and magazine stories. List wages along with pros and cons for jobs that interest you, so you can compare the jobs you're considering for career decision. Also consider collecting wage information about long-term work opportunities that you might choose in your future.

Compare large wage trends among different employers and work groups. There are small wage variations for the same job among different employers, with a few exceptions. Employers generally give promotions with small wage increases and with job title variations. So it's not meaningful to sort many of these small variations; instead compare the larger wage trends among different work groups and employers of interest.

Your wage level will tend to increase with work experience. Many employers give small raises and promotions annually or every few years. This creates small pay differences among the variations of job titles. Larger increases are gained by long-term employment within an organization, and by moving up the career ladder into higher level positions. Over time these wage increases make the "average pay" for work look much higher than you can expect for entry-level jobs. Compare wage trends for your job titles of interest, and also talk to workers about the wages and benefits in your choice of location.

Consider a benefits package as an important part of earnings. Some jobs have such high quality benefits and pensions that it's unnecessary to save much for retirement, so this adds great value to an ordinary income. All levels of jobs in government, such as police, firefighters and garbage collectors have high quality benefits for health insurance and pensions. Teachers and other educational workers also tend to have high quality benefits compared with many nongovernment jobs.

A strong benefits package greatly enhances ordinary wages. Focus on expensive benefits like pensions and health insurance when comparing work options. Many jobs don't provide pensions these days, or else they are being replaced with 401K saving programs that have very low value since employers contribute very little. If you have found work with very low pay, then it's impossible to afford savings for health insurance and a pension. Information about benefits can be difficult to find and changing occasionally, but your best source of up-to-date information is asking some workers who are currently employed in jobs and locations of your interest.

EDUCATION AND TESTING

Three Educational Levels
The vocational level of education is considered the lowest level of education for work. This level consists of a high school diploma or GED certificate. Occasionally job training programs are included with high school education. Or else job training may be available in one year programs. Otherwise on-the-job training is the most common procedure for this level of work.

Technical level jobs often require two-year college degrees, but this level may include some one-year programs. Occasionally four-year college degree programs are used for technical jobs such as engineering and science technicians, but these are often entry jobs for higher levels of professional work later. On-the-job training for this level of work is called an apprenticeship.

College level jobs require four years of education beyond high school, and this level includes jobs that require advanced college degrees, such as master's degrees, doctor's degrees and also specialized degrees for medicine and law. Advanced degrees require another two or three years of college study, so you need to plan ahead to earn suitable grades and test scores that are required to enter the advanced degree programs.

Advanced college degrees are required for occupations such as medical doctors, lawyers, college teachers and scientists. Master's degrees are required for social workers, librarians and counselors. Teachers in elementary and high school are often required to add a master's degree to update their teaching license, and business majors often add this higher level degree to advance into management positions.

Various educational levels can be used to work in some jobs, especially for technical level jobs, such as sales, entertainment, sports and the arts. You might find people with college degrees working in technical level jobs, especially for entry-level jobs. Also you might find people with vocational level education who obtain technical level jobs with experience. It's more efficient to sort job groups by their most common educational levels that are used for work. Then consider the variations of education you could use to qualify for the jobs you want.

Unusual educational programs may be found at the technical and college levels that lack suitability for most common jobs that are available. Unusual programs make it difficult to find work. Therefore choose your work preferences first, and then choose suitable education for your specific work goals.

Educational Levels and Job Categories

Compare job categories in the three common educational levels to identify your strongest interests for both education and work. See Appendix B for the SOC job categories arranged into three common educational levels. This arrangement provides a good introduction to work categories, while it helps to find educational levels and subject matter matching your work interests.

Job categories are arranged in a similar order for each level of education, beginning with the scientific and technical jobs and progressing towards the social science and artistic jobs. A group of engineering technicians has been added in the technical level categories to represent the new STEM jobs. This arrangement helps you explore related groups of jobs among all three levels, so this helps you find entry-level jobs, and then find higher level jobs that you might reach with greater work experience. This arrangement also helps you find all the related work options for each educational program that you may be considering.

Some job categories are located at several educational levels, since their educational requirements vary widely. For example, you can work at jobs in entertainment, music, agriculture and sales with many variations and levels of education. Some categories of work at the technical level may contain high level workers with college degrees. Whereas high level workers might be found working in alternate jobs such as management or teaching. Notice that the college level category of business management includes management jobs from all levels and categories of work, such as engineering, production, restaurant work, sales and protective services, etc.

Are you ready to pass the educational program and testing required for a job you want? Answer this question by exploring how work corresponds to education while you compare the categories and groups of jobs found at each educational level. Comparing work categories among all three educational levels helps you find the best educational options for your work goals. This helps to identify the testing requirements for your education and job choice, so you can begin preparing for these goals.

You can make better educational decisions by comparing job categories found in the three most common levels of education. Begin by sorting the largest job categories to understand your options comprehensively. Then find the SOC job categories or O*NET categories online where you can print your own copy showing the lower level job groups and titles for each category. Sort the categories and groups to find jobs that you prefer along with their related options so you can identify the best education to prepare for your future goals.

Preparing for Testing

Frequent testing can be expected throughout your school years, beginning in the lower grades with general achievement and proficiency testing. Then expect testing to enter some schools, to enter specific study programs at some schools, to pass study programs, to get licensed for professional jobs and also to get hired for some jobs. Try to identify long-term career interests, so you can begin preparing for the tests in your future.

If you know what testing to expect, you have the opportunity to prepare for testing. You can either choose a career that's suitable for your current level of test preparation, or else you can increase your test preparation for higher level goals.

Improve your test scores by studying carefully in school, by studying additional material on your own, by studying test practice guides and by taking test preparation classes. If you can identify the specific testing requirements for your goals, you can begin preparing to perform better on tests that you expect. Furthermore, your knowledge of the testing requirements can motivate you to be a better student and get better grades.

Often testing checks your general academic knowledge, so good school performance helps you perform better on advanced testing. Consider if your school covers the general academic knowledge sufficiently to meet your testing requirements. If your school program seems weak, then study suitable material on your own to prepare for testing. You might even attend a "prep school" instead of a regular high school. This provides some advantage in preparing for testing, since prep schools focus on preparation for the higher levels of education. Unfortunately you must pass a test to enter most prep schools, so your testing skills must be fairly good already.

College admissions testing such as the SAT and ACT is your most difficult testing in high school. Also additional testing may be required for admissions to specialized colleges and for special study programs at some colleges. Check what specific testing is required for your educational and work goals, so you have the opportunity to prepare to earn higher quality scores on testing. See Appendix A for a list of typical tests that are required for the most common options in education and work.

List all the testing you expect for education and work goals, and use the list to keep your focus on preparing for the testing. If you know about specific requirements for grades and testing to enter your choice of colleges and educational programs, then you have the opportunity to prepare for these testing occasions. Furthermore, if you know about a licensing test after your course of study, then you would study more carefully during the course to be ready for your testing.

Study test practice guides to improve your test taking skills and get "warm-up" practice. Sometimes practice guides clearly indicate what kinds of general or specialized knowledge you may expect on the testing, so you can improve your test scores by studying and reviewing that kind of subject matter. If you know that math and grammar questions are emphasized, you can focus on that material. You will find many test practice guides in libraries and bookstores, or else you can order these guides from the online web sites of publishers and bookstores.

Comparing Colleges and Expenses
There are three kinds of colleges with three levels of costs. Community colleges have two-year degree programs with the lowest cost. State colleges are considered nonprofit, and they offer comparatively lower costs for their residents. Large state colleges also have the largest selection of different educational programs and advanced degree programs to consider when you're looking for programs that match specific work interests. Whereas private colleges are known as "for profit" institutions, and they generally have the highest costs and also the highest entrance requirements in terms of high school grades and scores on the college admissions tests.

Compare costs for all colleges in this country with a recent copy of *The World Almanac*. It's worth checking if some colleges are offering scholarships to compete for students, and you might check what financial aid options are available to you. Consider that some colleges might provide free tuition if you're working there, even in a part-time job. Consider that some colleges may lack proper accreditation, so it's important to check if they have suitable quality accreditation or else their degree program won't be viewed favorably by employers.

Choose educational goals early during high school so you can work for the quality of grades you want for college. If your goals include an advanced college degree, you need a grade point average of B or higher during high school and college. Also you need to prepare for the college entrance testing and for any additional testing required to enter advanced degree programs. If you have poor grades in high school or else poor test scores on your college entrance exams, there might be another route to obtain more options for your college education.

You might begin study at your local community college if you have low grades in high school, and then transfer to a state college if your grades are satisfactory. If your grades continue to be good, you may transfer to any college that accepts you to finish your degree program. This route provides more options, but it limits your access to advanced degree programs unless you're earning high enough grades currently in college, since most colleges require a B grade average from your last degree program to enter their advanced programs.

Students don't realize what grades they need in high school until they begin applying to some colleges, and then it's too late. Generally, all private colleges require a grade average of B or higher in high school, and highly rated colleges require a grade point average of 3.5 or higher. Generally all colleges require a B average during college to enter advanced degree programs, and they require a B average during these programs to graduate. Also check about testing and written papers for advanced degree programs so you can prepare for these requirements.

If you need more time to get good grades during high school and college, then choose a smaller workload of study courses. Avoid taking too many courses that may result in lower grades. Also avoid taking extra activities that decrease your study time. Try limiting extra activity time to what best meets your schedule for earning the grades you want during high school and college. This provides enough time to study carefully and earn the quality of grade point average you need for future educational goals. Working students and those with learning disabilities can benefit from taking smaller workloads and also from tutoring.

Comparing the quality of educational programs among the colleges is fairly subtle. You can check the rankings in magazines and ask students about their experiences. College educational programs are usually ranked in terms of "the status of a school and its study program", and private colleges are ranked in terms of the prestige of their faculty. Some colleges are only highly ranked for specific programs. Find more information by talking to others, by checking web sites for colleges of interest, by reading college guide books, and then by calling the college registration offices with your remaining questions.

USING DECISION STRATEGIES

Career Decision Methods
* Inventory your skills and interests to identify strongest traits
* Consider educational interests to identify preferred options
* Write a comprehensive description of your personal traits and ideal job
* Compare pros and cons of your work interests with detailed career information
* Comparatively rank jobs you have selected as good options

The common method of career choice is sorting the options in education and work to identify all of your strongest preferences. This method is usually done anyway along with other methods, except that you can simply choose this way without using the other decision methods. Most students will prefer using several methods, especially if they have difficulty with their decision.

The primary strategy for career decision is using inventories of interests and skills to identify personal traits that correspond to job requirements. For help with this process, the O*NET web site provides information about work abilities and interest areas. This web site shows sixteen career clusters corresponding to the profiles of worker abilities and interests. Each cluster shows the jobs of successful workers who have the interests and abilities represented by the group profile. Try to identify what group of abilities and interests is the best match for you, and then see the corresponding job clusters that match these traits.

Comprehensive orientation information about jobs is the most important requirement for finding your strongest interests. Begin with orientation information that's reasonably thorough and well organized to reach sufficient understanding about the options. Then you may sort specific options in the large categories and groups, and weigh these options and find your strongest preferences in terms of both education and work.

Academic performance and educational interests are good indicators of your best possibilities. Try to identify your preferred level of education and subject matter. Explore work categories among all three educational levels in Appendix B to find your strongest interests for education and work. Most work categories have both higher and lower level jobs with different educational requirements, so you might begin working with lower level jobs and continue adding work experience to reach higher levels of work. Try to identify both current and long-term interests and choose work in terms of a larger group that provides some flexibility for working in various kinds of related jobs.

List all the options you definitely want to consider, so you can compare these options with detailed information. Comparing the pros and cons of your listed options helps you identify your strongest preferences in terms of work and educational options. Also list related and alternative jobs that you might work in with your choices of work and education, since this helps you identify and prepare for more flexible options.

Try to use your strongest interests and abilities in a career. Consider what talents and interests are revealed by activities that you prefer most. What conversational topics are you drawn towards, how do others see your talents and interests, and what activities are you the most likely to be doing in your spare time?

Organize notes about your interests and abilities to identify your personal traits. Compare your written notes with the interests and abilities listed for job groups found on the O*NET web site. Most career advisors will agree that you should apply your strongest interests and abilities towards job choice, since this contributes the most towards your long-term success.

Alternative Decision Method

Write a comprehensive description of your traits and ideal job. Describe your personal interests and abilities and what activities you prefer most. Organize your notes and lists so you can easily use this information to design a job matching your description of traits. Then if you can't find this kind of job in the marketplace, you might create this job opportunity by starting a business that provides this kind of work for you. Otherwise you might try to sell your services to any business that can benefit from your unique description of traits and skills.

The disadvantage of "designing your own job" is that unusual work opportunities are difficult to find. In other words, it might be too challenging to find this kind of work in the marketplace or else to start your own business using your designed job.

Try to estimate your opportunity for finding work in a job you might create with this method of career choice. Also look for similar or related jobs that form a bridge to your preferred work. It's always wise to have alternative job options in mind that you can use for backup if your first choice isn't working well. Good options for alternative work should be similar to your designed job so they provide some experience for your primary work.

Keep your list of preferred alternative jobs handy if you have chosen a challenging career in terms of finding employment. Challenging careers are those that depend too much on luck or unique talent for success, or else they are scarcely available. Often you won't know if you have enough luck or unique talent until it's too late to prepare for another job. When choosing a career with scarce opportunities or one that depends too much upon luck, it's wise to prepare for an alternative job option that you can use for backup work.

Challenging careers to manage are found in entertainment, sports, art, starting your own business, and anything else very challenging or unpredictable to be reasonably certain this will work well for you. You can add career security by choosing one or more backup jobs that provides comfortable alternative work. Ideally, your backup job should keep you working close to your preferred career, so this job might create a stepping-stone into your preferred career at some point. A good back-up job would provide related experience for your primary goal.

Listing Alternative Options

List all work options that you would prefer for alternative jobs, and save your list for a rainy day when you can't find a job in your first choice of work. Use alternative jobs for backup when you have difficulty finding work, or if you want to try different work, or if you change your mind about your first choice of job. You might keep your list handy during job hunting to identify work possibilities that you can use whenever you find interesting alternative jobs available. Save your list so you won't need to go through the job sorting process again, you can simply change to another job option on your list.

If you want to advance in your career with work experience, you need to avoid using alternative jobs, but you might want to keep a list of alternative job possibilities handy for a rainy day. When the job marketplace is weak for your primary job choice, then you will have a greater sense of security about job hunting if you have listed some alternative work options that provide a reasonable income, at least on a temporary basis.

Alternative jobs are useful for temporary work when you have difficulty finding work. Instead of being unemployed for a long time during a lengthy job search, look for temporary work in alternative jobs that are easier to obtain. Your list of alternative options can provide flexibility for keeping yourself consistently employed when your preferred job becomes difficult to find.

Vocational level jobs are easy to obtain for alternative work, especially if they don't require specific skills or work experience. Technical level jobs generally require working in related jobs of your career area or else showing an interest in learning other variations of work. For workers with advanced college degrees, the typical alternative jobs are teaching and management. Usually this means teaching in high school or college, and the management jobs might be found in educational administration or in your specific field of education.

Lacking Strong Interests

Career choice is easy when you have strong interests and skills. Your career stands out, and you might not bother learning about the other options with career information. Otherwise you need help sorting the options with comprehensive career information. If you lack strong interests, it's possible that sorting all of the options might not help you locate any definite preferences. Therefore the only strategy left is listing and ranking your options to select what seems like a comparatively best option.

If you have very wide interests and abilities or if you lack strong specific interests and talents, you can focus on other considerations to weigh for career decision. It's wise to place more emphasis on the marketplace requirements and choose a career with more work opportunities. You might focus on finding work with better wages or retirement benefits. You might look for a better employment outlook in your choice of location, or look for work that's widely available in many different locations. You might also consider looking for a good employment outlook for any future promotions that you may be seeking, so that your planning includes these options as well.

If your career decision isn't clear after a reasonable amount of sorting and thinking about options, this indicates that you don't have strong interests and preferences. Your interests may be widely scattered or you may lack definite talents that match any one career. When career decision is unusually difficult, you can simply make a tentative decision that could be modified later if your interests become clear enough to seek a career change. Try various methods to explore your interests and traits fully. Then rank job options you want to consider, and comparatively choose an option that seems most reasonable to you.

In the past, the top four careers for men were engineering, medicine, law and business (mostly accounting). The top careers for women were teaching, nursing, librarian and social work. Today you need to focus on job market demand in order to find sufficient opportunities for work. Compare information about the job market outlook when ranking your options, and then choose your best option even though you might not like all of the job features. If you simply cannot decide about career choice, prepare for the most reasonable option that can keep you working until you find your larger mission in life or discover if you have any stronger interests to pursue.

If you don't have strong interests and talents, it's worth identifying some alternative jobs, since you can't compete as well for work in your career area. Identify the related jobs in your career area that might provide different variations of work experience or working in different settings. This creates more possibilities during job hunting and later for changing jobs. Sort the pros and cons of your listed possibilities so you can find what options are likely to work best for you. Collect information to identify your concerns and rank your preferred options.

Leave Time for Thinking

Generally you can make better decisions by taking more time for thinking. Begin by collecting and organizing the information you want to use for comparing options. Organize notes for long-term thinking and occasionally review your notes for thinking about these options until you can reach a decision with reasonable certainty. Don't wait for your decision to simply arrive someday.

It works better to continue gathering information and thinking about your alternative options occasionally.

Your brain continues to process information even when you're not aware of it, so eventually you will see a solution emerging. Often this is described as "sleeping on it". Letting some time pass, along with occasionally reconsidering your information, helps your brain reach complex decisions because more time is available for processing information thoroughly. Leave as much time as you reasonably can for thinking about complex decisions like career choice, since the extra time for thinking increases your opportunity for reaching a better quality decision.

If you're having difficulty with career decision, prepare for the most reasonable option that can keep you employed until you discover any stronger goals or talent. If your interests are highly diversified and don't match any work options, you can simply rank your possibilities and decide in terms of current market conditions. Career choice doesn't need to satisfy all of your interests. This choice simply can be one of your better options until you discover any stronger interests to pursue.

ISSUES FOR YOUR DECISION

Timing Educational Goals
Significant advantages are possible by starting college education immediately after high school, whereas delaying your higher education for work has some disadvantages. Later you might not have parental support handy to attend school full time. Also it's difficult to leave work and return to school after you have become dependent upon an income, or else if you have started to support other family members.

Time scheduling is the biggest problem with starting college education later. You can attend college part time while working full time, but this combination may be difficult to schedule so it takes much longer to finish your education. The other option is attending college full time while working part time, but this leaves less time for your best quality study and good grades. Most students prefer full-time college as soon as possible after high school, while others may prefer to work their way through college slowly with either full or part-time work.

Several advantages are possible by delaying college study or else by proceeding slowly through college. If you're academically unprepared for college but you want higher levels of education, you can benefit from proceeding more slowly through college. Also if you want better quality grades and learning from difficult college courses, it's better to proceed slowly through college by taking smaller work loads of study courses. Students who have learning disabilities can get better results by proceeding slowly through college along with getting help from tutoring.

You might consider delaying higher education, since you will have more interest and maturity for study when you're older. Occasionally this strategy works well, but it tends to conflict with other interests and goals later in life. You might have acquired a family or a household to support by age thirty, and then it's very difficult to manage a challenging study program by proceeding slowly through college. You need to consider what time schedule will work best for your own interests by comparing the options and weighing the pros and cons in terms of personal priorities and preferences.

Financial Security and Independence
Your personal security in terms of employment and income may depend on job choice, educational preparation and continuously building competitive work experience. Many jobs are specialized today, so you must have specific education and work experience to compete for them successfully.

Women's lifestyles today often require independent financial roles, and this requires dependable careers and income. As you become aware of the risks in life, you will realize the importance of being self-supporting or else adding to a household income. You might have the misfortune of your partner leaving, dying, losing a job, becoming disabled or just not earning enough income from a job. Then you must help to earn a living or else fully support a household by yourself.

Women are expected to contribute to their household income today, or else they must be totally self-supporting. Even taking time off for family duties has been shown to cause difficulty for women in finding work again. Taking time off means less work experience on your resume, so you can't compete well in a weak job market with other resumes that show more work experience. Often you can't compete well for the typical promotions in your career area after having taken time off for family duties.

There are greater quantities of single parent families today, so you might need sufficient income to support your household. Otherwise you might choose work simply to add more income to your household, since many jobs are low paying and it often takes more than one income to support a household. Consider that you must contribute payments to social security for about ten years of work approximately to become eligible for these pension benefits. Check the social security work requirements so you can plan for security with this retirement pension and also this disability plan.

Your future financial security begins with career planning, since most people must be self-supporting all their lives. Your employment security begins with preparing for a reasonable job at the typical age of financial independence, and this requires adequate information about work options, education options and the current employment outlook in the marketplace. Plan for future financial security by comparing income and employment outlook for work options that you're considering. Obtain greater financial security by choosing a career area with a good outlook for work and by choosing suitable education.

Considering Job Market Changes

Some jobs are increasing in employment opportunities while others are becoming obsolete. Therefore it's important to find information about what jobs are going unfilled in the market. Check the outlook for large categories of work, in addition to checking for specific jobs, so you can choose suitable education to prepare for work with good opportunities for employment.

Work is becoming more mechanized and computerized today, so greater numbers of technicians are needed, while simple labor jobs are declining. Education jobs are also increasing, since more students are seeking education to prepare for work that requires greater knowledge. Health care jobs are also increasing today, since the elderly are living longer and using more health care.

Jobs requiring knowledge of science, technology, engineering and math are known as STEM jobs. These jobs represent work categories with the fastest growing employment, and one half of these new tech jobs don't require four year college degrees. Unfortunately, schools are failing to provide information about what jobs are in greatest demand and failing to prepare students for new technology jobs with the most opportunities.

You might consider placing more emphasis on finding work with reasonably good wages and good outlook for employment, instead of looking for work that you prefer most. Statistics show that many jobs don't pay well enough for a worker to live alone with a good standard of living. Wages have been going down to compete with the global economy while the cost of living has been going up for housing, cars and energy.

Workers expect to earn an adequate income to buy a house and car, or to rent good housing and be fully self-supporting. However as living costs continue to rise while wages stay low, it's clear that many workers cannot earn sufficient income to buy a house and car. Likewise, many retired people cannot afford a middle class lifestyle. Today, people with low incomes must live with relatives or in group homes so they can share the growing costs of housing, energy and transportation.

Today workers are facing greater risks in terms of losing jobs and having low wages because of technology changes and business restructuring. It might be necessary to move around for work or else live with relatives during the time it takes to find another job. Couples often find that both of them must work to support a household. Therefore an important goal with career planning is getting enough information about earnings and job outlook in order to find work that provides reasonable security from very low income and unemployment.

Moving Along a Career Ladder

Choose a life long sequence of what you hope to achieve with your career instead of simply choosing one job for right now. Planning ahead for long-term goals helps you avoid getting "stuck in a rut" without good future options. Your higher level positions on the career ladder may require more educational preparation. Explore related job options in all three levels of education to find your best entry jobs and then to find higher level jobs that you might seek later during your career.

Plan for education and work experience you need to advance towards your long-term career goals. Don't count on automatic promotions as a natural course of events during your working years. Instead identify the higher level positions you want to reach during your career, and plan for the education and work experience that's required for each kind of promotion.

Prepare for your long-term work goals and future promotions before you begin working, so you won't need to return to school. Then you can focus on obtaining suitable work experience you need to prepare for the job promotions you might want later. Begin by choosing suitable entry jobs for your long-term goals, and then look for opportunities to advance with suitable job positions and work experience that can help you move along the path to your long-term career goals.

Although you might get lucky and be in the right place at the right time, it's better to plan for preferred promotions by seeking relevant education and work experience. Take advantage of any on-the-job opportunities to obtain the work skills and experience needed to prepare for future promotions. Many careers provide the opportunity to advance into management positions with long-term work experience if you demonstrate the appropriate skills during your job promotions.

It's wise to keep up with the current workplace trends and changes in your career area. Keep up with business news for your career, and talk with coworkers and local people about the current workplace trends. This helps you prepare better to take advantage of the opportunities for your preferred promotions.

Estimate what kind of work experience you will need to position yourself for promotions in your current place of employment. When you keep informed about the current opportunities in your work category, you can try to take advantage of preferred job openings as they become available in your location.

Getting Information from Workers
Supplement career information from books with talking to people who are currently working in your jobs and locations of interest. Information in current career books may be inadequate, so it's better to supplement job information with practical material from people working in particular jobs and locations. It's the best reason for networking before choosing your career. Only current workers in specific jobs and locations know some forms of practical information, and not all workers are knowledgeable. Discuss your concerns with various workers, and also seek "second hand" information from people who may have heard worthwhile information about jobs that interest you.

Practical information from other workers is often overlooked, but it's very important for improving your current functioning and long-term progress. Information from workers is useful in several ways for better quality career functioning. This kind of information helps with decision-making when choosing a career. Later it helps with functioning better while working in a career, and finally it helps with moving up the career ladder into your preferred sequence of higher positions.

When you discuss job concerns with other workers, you can learn about current work requirements and problems that you should consider for career progress. You can learn information about the work place that helps you perform better on-the-job and helps you prepare for promotions. Information from other workers contributes to functioning more effectively in your work and to getting along better with coworkers. It's an important activity for promoting greater career growth.

Collect notes about worthwhile information you learn, or else the material may become partially or totally forgotten instead of growing into a larger picture. Write your notes privately so you don't intimidate speakers during your informal interview. Your casual discussion with other workers might provide important information that helps you perform better in your current job, and that provides advantages for gaining higher level positions in your current or future workplace.

The only disadvantage of secondhand job information is your need to weigh individual bias and the unique qualities of specific workplaces. Realize that other workers' viewpoints might not match your own views and attitudes within the same situation.

Consider that specific workplaces may have unique problems that are different from other locations with the same jobs. Weigh subjective opinions versus factual data to evaluate workers' views compared to your own outlook. Also, try to ask questions of various people who may provide different views. In spite of these limitations, gathering practical information is worthwhile to improve your current functioning at work and to facilitate your long-term career growth.

List your questions as they occur to you, and save them for an opportunity to ask others about their own work experiences. By gathering questions, you can avoid browsing with only vague questions, and you can avoid incidentally discovering important information about jobs. You might begin asking questions about the working conditions, benefits and salary. You might discuss what experience is required for the typical promotions, and ask about opportunities for on-the-job training.

JOB SEARCH STEPS

Job Hunting Methods

* Go into local businesses and fill out job applications
* Call preferred businesses to ask about job openings
* Network or ask people if they know about job openings
* Apply on company web sites and general career web sites
* List resume online with regional or national career web sites
* Go into government web sites or offices to check openings
* Check state employment services and community groups
* Apply to ads in newspapers and professional magazines
* Apply to employment agencies that specialize in your work
* Check with your college career office for the first entry job
* Consider your current opportunities for entrepreneurship

Many students are working to pay for their college education, so a summary of job hunting and application is included here. Begin your job hunting by listing preferred workplaces first, and then by listing the job hunting methods you want to use.

The primary method of job hunting is simply going around to your local businesses and asking about job openings and filling out applications. Bring your personal information and reference list so you can fill out applications. Some businesses may prefer resumes, so take along copies of your resume to hand out. Going around filling out applications works better for lower level manufacturing and service jobs, while resumes are preferred for higher level and professional jobs.

Your favorite companies might never advertise job openings when they are getting enough walk-in applications. Make your first applications by walking into nearby and favorite companies of interest, since your nearby jobs make it easy to get to work. Then make walk-in applications at the second level of companies you prefer most, before using remaining methods of job hunting to search more widely for your preferred kind of work.

Many job openings are not advertised immediately, so it's worthwhile calling and asking about job openings or else simply walking in to apply for work. New openings are likely to be filled by people applying on their own, or else by people who have heard about openings from current employees when networking to find more opportunities for employment.

"Networking" or asking people if they know about any job openings is another method of searching for jobs, and people might tell you about any openings in their workplace or openings they have heard about. Try the school career office if you have recently finished school. They may have established connections with employers who are looking for recent graduates, and your first job is more difficult to get without work experience.

Today most job openings are placed online on the company web site or on local career web sites. First make applications on web sites of companies that interest you most. Then use your regional career web sites or else national web sites to search more widely. If the specific job is more important to you than the location, use large national career web sites to post your resume and to apply for your choice of job openings.

An ideal employment service would be a "jobs clearinghouse" for all local jobs in each region. This service would show all the jobs currently available for each region. Job seekers could list their resume with this service, and they could describe the work and location they prefer. No doubt regional career web sites try to provide this kind of service, but they probably don't get all of the job openings so it's necessary to search in various other ways to find more opportunities.

You can partially create a regional jobs clearinghouse service for yourself. Select your preferred location and list all of the local employers where you could apply for work. First apply to those employers you prefer most. If you lack results, apply to your second choice of employers, etc., until all of your options have been explored. Your local Chamber of Commerce probably has a list of the larger companies in your location, and many small businesses are listed in your local phone book yellow pages or you can simply drive around and look for local businesses.

Get better results by using numerous job search methods, especially if the job market is weak for your career or location.

Begin with the most common methods and consider that some companies prefer online applications. If you haven't found work with the common methods of application, consider placing your resume online. It's helpful to realize that employment agencies prefer to place workers with specific skills and experiences, so that specialized agencies are more likely to find work for you.

The biggest problem with job-hunting is finding work when the general job market is weak. You can expect to struggle with preparing large quantities of applications and waiting a long time to get hired. Listing your resume on large career web sites might not produce job offers when the job market is weak, so you might be waiting and applying long-term. Use a general resume most of the time to make more applications, and only tailor your resume for highly preferred job opportunities.

Steps for Basic Resume

Personal Information – name, address, phone number and email address

Job Objective – job title or category of work you want

Experience - work experience listed in chronological order with your most recent job first

Education – degrees or diplomas listed with recent one first

References – list three or four references on a separate page, and this page is only provided upon request

Optional Resume Steps

Skills Summary – list your skills by relevant categories if you lack work experience

Licenses and Awards – if relevant for the specific job

Personal information is the first category, but leave off the category title and center your information at the top of the first page or arrange it like a business letterhead. Never include some kinds of personal information like your date of birth and social security number. This kind of information is only provided to employers after you have been hired, and it's written on the forms filled out at work by new employees.

Job objective states the job title for your application, or else this might be a one-paragraph summary of your general work goals and skills. This kind of summary also makes a good first paragraph in your cover letter, so you might leave this off your resume when you're sending a cover letter.

List work experience and education in chronological order, beginning with the most recent ones first. Use category titles like those in the list above. List dates of employment with addresses and phone numbers, and possibly your job manager's name if requested. If you have very few work experience entries, then space out each entry into three or four lines. If you have many entries, only list recent and relevant experience. If you have licenses and awards relevant for the job, add another category for these. Create a one page resume, and consider using a resume template for a professional looking result.

If you lack work experience, use the "Summary of Skills" category on your resume to describe your relevant work skills. This summary uses short lists or paragraphs to describe your skills under headings such as Customer Service Skills, Problem-Solving Skills, Communication Skills, Computer Skills, Research Skills and Organizational Skills. Choose the appropriate category titles for skills preferred for the kind of work you seek.

If you want security for personal information with your online resume, leave off your name, address and phone number. Only provide an email address from a service like "yahoo", with a nice nickname so that any contacts must provide their identity first. This gives you an opportunity to check if this is a legitimate employer that you would be interested in working for before you reply to them about setting up a job interview.

Writing a Cover Letter

A typical cover letter consists of one page with three paragraphs. The first paragraph is an introduction stating what job you're applying for and summarizing your traits and interests.

The middle paragraph or two of your cover letter may present detailed information to enhance what's included in your resume about skills, knowledge and experience. If your resume contains a "summary of skills", add some detailed material about your qualifications. Your middle paragraphs should provide additional focused information about personal traits and experiences that are relevant. It's an opportunity to place an emphasis upon your strongest traits that are most relevant for the job.

Summarize your strengths for the job in the last paragraph, also you may tell about your availability for the job interview. Both the first and last paragraphs should summarize personal strengths, interests and suitability for the job. Don't repeat the same sentences, but instead create variations of sentences when you want to emphasize your strongest key points.

Tailor your description of skills and knowledge to match the traits requested by the employer, especially if these traits are somewhat different from the kind of work your application is designed for generally. Save all variations of your cover letters and resumes in computer files, since you may only need about ten to twenty variations for all of your job applications.

Write one general cover letter and resume for your largest category of job applications. Then write additional versions for your most frequent variations of job applications. For all other applications, simply compose small variations as you go along. Save copies of various cover letters in your computer word files. Also save copies of resume variations that you have created, so you can print copies for similar job applications, but you need to change the company name and address for each application.

Listing Your References

Ask some acquaintances to be your job references before leaving your current school or work setting. References can be teachers when leaving school, except that it's very rare for entry jobs to ask for references from past teachers. When leaving a job, ask workplace associates to be your references. Later these people might be difficult to locate, or they might not remember you well enough to provide a good reference. It's more efficient to arrange references before leaving your current setting.

Generally your resume, cover letter and reference list should be one page each, with a list of three or four people on your reference page. This page could contain phone numbers, and the name of a workplace or school for each reference. First get their approval before using a home address, phone or email address. Don't include your reference page with job applications unless it's specifically requested. This page is only provided upon request, usually during an interview, so remember to bring this page along to job interviews.

A few professional jobs require prewritten reference letters that you must provide along with your job application or else upon request at an interview. If your job requires it, ask your choice of people for these letters before moving from one setting to another. Try to develop good quality references by making a good impression on teachers, coworkers and managers.

Organizing Interview Notes

You won't be speechless when job interview questions are asked if you have previously outlined answers for the typical questions you might expect. When you prepare answers for the common job interview questions, this helps you deal with many variations of similar questions. When your answers for interview questions are outlined or listed as phrases grouped with labels, they're easy to review and remember. Also include some ideas about stories you might use to describe skill building experiences.

List your traits in terms of knowledge, skills and experience. Organize your lists into groups for easy review of listed traits before going to job interviews and even writing job applications. Also prepare information or stories about your skill building experiences, just in case an interviewer asks for examples and wants more detailed information about your experiences.

Study the qualifications requested by each employer before writing cover letters and preparing for interviews. Your answers should emphasize that you have specific skills and experiences matching an employer's description of the traits being sought. Review your listed traits before writing each cover letter for job applications, and place your focus on the skills and experiences that each specific employer has requested.

Emphasize your strongest traits for the job before presenting interesting stories about work experience. The amount of detail provided in cover letters and interviews should be flexible, so that it varies with the amount you wish to write or the amount of time you're provided to answer interview questions. Summarize your traits for cover letters and job interviews before adding detailed material. Summarize qualifications for introductions and conclusions in your cover letters and interviews.

It's unnecessary to memorize interview notes, because the exercise of preparing notes and reviewing them tends to produce good quality speaking during an interview. However if you want to memorize important points in your notes, reduce each point to a key word and make sentences with these key words. If the information that you're using for interviews and cover letters is well organized, the key words will jog your memory.

Practice both verbally and by writing answers for questions that you might expect in job interviews. When you only practice verbally, you will tend to forget your excellent answers. Review your list of traits and answers to common interview questions before each job interview. Also review any notes about detailed stories that you could use during interviews. If the interviewer appears to want more material than you have prepared, tell stories about your practical experiences and about how you have solved problems relevant for your kind of work.

For higher level job interviews, practice your answers verbally with someone asking you the questions for warm-up exercises. Don't worry if you start out sounding weak. Just keep practicing until your answers are good enough or significantly improved. You can find practice questions in job interview books to help you prepare answers for the most common interview questions and even for some unusual questions. Before each interview, simply review your written answers and listed traits.

If asked a vague question, such as "Tell me about yourself", by an interviewer, describe your education and work experience. Use your understanding of the job requirements to describe traits that show your suitability for the job. Generally summarize your material first when answering job interview questions. If the interviewer appears to want more information, continue adding detailed description about your qualifications and specific experiences according to the time provided.

If your interview includes a social occasion like a luncheon meeting with a group of people, write notes to plan suitable questions to ask your future colleagues who are participating. Also plan for suitable introductions and closing remarks and for pleasant conversational topics, in addition to your summary and thank you at the end of an interview. Planning should help you prepare better quality material and avoid the wrong topics and poor quality material during these occasions.

Show a friendly and positive attitude about the interviewer, the job and yourself. Showing a positive attitude presents the kind of attitude and people skills that most employers want. Some people claim it works to simply ask for the job, but you need to use your own judgment about the situation if this might work well for you or else if this might have any negative effect upon your prospects of getting the job offer you want. Instead of simply asking for the job, your interview performance should show good salesmanship. Essentially, only say positive things about your traits and skills and work experience.

Send a thank you letter or email summarizing your strengths after important job interviews. Your "thank you" letter should reinforce the interviewer's attention on your qualifications so that you may get more consideration. Sending the follow-up thank you letter provides your opportunity to call more attention to yourself and your skills. You can summarize your traits and strengths for the job, and you can draw more positive attention to yourself and your job application.

Planning your future begins with good orientation information about education and work, so you can identify your options and find those options you prefer most. Although career planning strategies can help with sorting your preferences for education and work, in the final analysis you need to list your reasonable options, then research and rank them to find your strongest possibilities. Some practical steps for exploring your preferences in education and work are listed below.

Steps For Educational Planning

List and rank your educational interests

Consider what level of education you want to obtain

Consider your grades and test scores for educational goals

High school grades are your best predictor of college grades

What scores can you expect on college entrance tests?

What personal achievements do you value the most?

List your preferences for reading, hobbies and activities

Do you prefer scholarly or physical activities?

Describe your greatest source of satisfaction from activities

List the educational programs and colleges you prefer

List all of the work options that you would consider

What kind of work interests you the most?

How would you describe your ideal job?

What qualities are you looking for in your future work?

What kind of work qualifications do you want to develop?

What are your strengths and weaknesses for work goals?

What are some things that you find difficult to do?

How would you define a pleasant work environment?

Consider what locations and work environments you prefer

Research your listed work options to identify preferences

Weigh the pros and cons of your listed work options

Rank your list of options to identify strongest preferences

Identify several related work opportunities for each job

List all of the work opportunities for your choice of education

List alternative work opportunities for your educational goals

Prepare for suitable school performance to reach your goals

Prepare for testing to reach both education and work goals

Keep track of job market changes when planning work goals

APPENDIX A

Examples of Testing for Education and Work

Elementary Level

Achievement Tests – for selected grade levels and subjects

Proficiency Tests – to pass selected grade levels

High School Level

Entrance Exams – to enter special high schools and prep schools

Proficiency Tests – to pass grade levels and graduate high school

GED – certificate instead of the high school diploma

PSAT – preliminary college entrance exams during high school

Advanced Placement Tests for college credit in various subjects

College Level

Exams such as SAT and ACT and CLEP taken in high school

Advanced College Levels

Entrance Exams to enter Advanced Degree programs, MAT, GRE

Entrance Exams for Law, Medical, Business: LSAT, MCAT, GMAT

Exit Exams and Written Papers for Advanced Degree programs

Entrance Testing for Vocational Level Jobs

Computer Tests for Office Workers, Commercial Drivers License,
Civil Service Tests for Postal Workers and many government jobs,
Military Entrance, Tests of Basic Skills used for some occupations

Entrance Testing for Technical Level Programs

Police, Firefighter, Military Technologist, Air Traffic Controller

License Testing for Technical Level Careers

Airplane Pilot, Ship Captain, Railroad Engineer, Building Contractor,
Computer Technician Certifications, HVAC Technician, Electrician,
Mechanic, Plumber, Stockbroker, Real Estate Broker, Appraiser, Barber,
Beautician, Licensed Practical Nurse, Diagnostic Technicians, Various
Health Therapists and Emergency Medical Technicians

License Testing for College Level Careers

Medical Doctors, Dentists, Pharmacists, Opticians, Veterinarians,
Registered Nurses, Medical Therapists, State Bar Exam for Attorneys,
CPA Test for Accountants, Teachers License Exam in many states,
Social Workers, Engineers and Architects (licensing is optional)

APPENDIX B

SOC Job Categories by Educational Levels

COLLEGE LEVEL JOB CATEGORIES

Architects and Engineers

Computer Scientists and Mathematicians

Life, Physical and Social Scientists

Management Occupations (All job categories)

Business & Financial Occupations

Legal Occupations

Healthcare Practitioners

Education, Training and Library

Community and Social Services

Design & Arts, Entertainment, Sports, Media

TECHNICAL LEVEL JOB CATEGORIES

Engineering, Science & Computer Technicians

Installation, Maintenance and Repair

Production Technologies Workers

Construction & Extraction Technologies

Transportation and Material Moving

Farming, Fishing and Forestry

Protective Services; Guards, Police & Firefighters

Military Technologies; Air, Water & Land Services

Healthcare Technologists and Technicians

Sales and Related Workers

Office, Administrative Support & Managers

Education, Community and Social Service Aides

Design & Arts, Entertainment, Sports, Media

Personal Care Service

Food Preparation

VOCATIONAL LEVEL JOB CATEGORIES

Installation, Maintenance and Repair

Production Workers

Construction & Extraction Workers

Transportation and Material Moving

Farming, Fishing and Forestry

Protective Services; Guards and Firefighters

Military Enlisted Occupations

Healthcare Support Workers

Sales and Related Workers

Office and Administrative Support

Building and Grounds Cleaning & Maintenance

Personal Care and Service

Food Preparation and Service

REFERENCES

Adler, Mortimer and Charles Van Doren. *How to Read a Book*, New York: Simon & Schuster, 1972. (Analytical Reading)

Flippo, R.F. and D.C.Caverly, eds. *Handbook of College Reading and Study Strategy Research*, New York: Lawrence Erlbaum Associates Publishers, 2000.

Joyce, Bruce and Marsha Weil with Emily Calhoun. *Models of Teaching, Sixth Edition*, Boston: Allyn and Bacon, 2000. (Steps for the methods of teaching)

Legasto, Augusto jr., Jay Forrester and James Lyneis. *System Dynamics*, New York: North-Holland Publishing Company, 1980.

McKeachie, Wilbert J. *Teaching Tips: A Guidebook for the Beginning College Teacher, Eighth Edition*, Massachusetts: D.C. Heath and Company, 1986. (This edition has teaching methods and techniques)

Richardson, Virginia, ed. *Handbook of Research on Teaching, Fourth Edition*, Washington D.C.: American Education Research Association, 2001.

Robinson, Adam. *What Smart Students Know*, New York: Crown Publishers, 1993. (Cyber Learning)

Senge, Peter et al. *Schools that Learn,* New York: Random House, 2000. (System Dynamics applied in the schools)

Sikula, John, sr. ed. *Handbook of Research on Teachers Education, Second Edition*, New York: Simon & Schuster Macmillan, 1996.

ABOUT THE AUTHOR

Jen McCall has a master's degree in educational psychology and teaching experience at several intermediate elementary levels. She performed volunteer work for a local association for learning disabilities, and worked for her local college where a deficiency of resources was observed for improving studying and teaching. Strategies in this study guide are the result of her lifelong hobby of exploring study strategies and teaching methods that help both students and teachers improve their quality of functioning.

Made in the USA
Middletown, DE
09 September 2022